PRAISE *for*

THE RED RIBBON

"*The Red Ribbon* is an unflinching account of loss and the resiliency of the often-complicated bond of love. The prose and poetry are lucid and lovely, the tale honestly told. But beyond the particulars of this very personal memoir, Bills tells a story that is not merely factual, but true. While every death and every grief is unique, anyone who has journeyed through the maelstrom of loss, especially sudden, unexpected loss, will recognize the territory Bills describes. One will read it and feel less alone."
—Rev. Jill Job Saxby, JD, MDiv, First Congregational Church, UCC, South Portland, Maine

"Nancy Bills's *The Red Ribbon* is a compelling account of unexpected loss. The reader is invited to accompany Bills on grief's journey. As a recent widow, I found her memoir comforting and helpful. For readers who have suffered loss, it is an important read."
—Susan Dahlgren Daigneault, EdD, author of *In the Shadow of a Mountain: A Soldier's Struggle with PTSD*

"Nancy Freund Bills has captured the pain of great loss without sentimentality. *The Red Ribbon,* a beautifully written memoir, tells a tender and tragic story of courage."
—Ruth Townsend Story, MA, author and writing teacher at Osher Lifelong Learning Institute at University of Southern Maine

"An amazing accomplishment offering help and hope to others suffering losses . . . Bills's work, which is infused with pain and grace, moves into emotional country most fear to explore. She shares generously the truth of her experience, and the reader is stunned, brought to tears, and needs to be reminded to breathe."
—Walden S. Morton, editor of 2017 Maine Literary Awards Anthology finalist *KALEIDOSCOPE*

"A brave memoir about a family's heartbreaking journey of grief and healing."
—Shelagh Ramage Forland, LCSW, MSW, child and family therapist

"A bolt of lightning . . . an incision in time. The grief that ensues is richly told, poetically nuanced, and intimately revealed in the beautiful memoir of trauma, love, and healing."
—Mary E. Plouffe, author of *I Know It in My Heart: Walking Through Grief with a Child*

"A heartfelt story of love and loss, rendered in clear and beautiful prose. Its music will resonate in your heart long after you're finished reading."
—Richard Cass, 2018 Maine Literary Awards winner and author of the Elder Darrow Mystery series

THE
RED RIBBON

THE
RED RIBBON

A MEMOIR

BY

NANCY FREUND BILLS

SHE WRITES PRESS

Published 2019
Printed in the United States of America
ISBN: 978-1-63152-573-5
ISBN: 978-1-63152-574-2
Library of Congress Control Number: 2018953149

For information, address:
She Writes Press
1569 Solano Ave #546
Berkeley, CA 94707

She Writes Press is a division of SparkPoint Studio, LLC.

Book design by Stacey Aaronson

FOR MY SONS—

WITH MY LOVE AND PROFOUND RESPECT

"Tho' much is taken, much abides..."
by Alfred, Lord Tennyson

CONTENTS

PART II: MY SEASON OF DEATH

AUTHOR'S NOTE

Readers most often ask me if *The Red Ribbon* is true. Yes. It is. However, I want to share with my readers that I wrote the stories, the chapters, one at a time. Each bubbled up in my mind and heart determined to be written. And only later did I arrange them in a semblance of chronological order. Still, many important events and even significant people are omitted. And the order remains tangential.

The writing process was painful. As I wrote, I cried and laughed. One way I was able to find the courage I needed was to assign everyone in my stories different names. My sons became Simon and Teddy; my husband became Geoff, a name I'm sure he would have liked. And I gave us the family name of Green, a promise that our family would survive and grow. I wanted to hold out hope. (Only the animals, Charlie, the beagle, and Mark, the gray thoroughbred, retain their own names. And me, I'm Nancy.)

I need to confess that there are still unwritten chapters, events too painful to tackle now. Maybe sometime. But maybe not. Some readers are curious about where I began. I wrote "The Emptying and Filling of the Drawer" first (in 2001) when I was taking a memoir class at the University of Southern Maine. And I wrote "Gentle to Market" last (in 2016) for a writing workshop; it was tough going. Close to the end, I wrote "Atonement," and the confession of my regrets was good for my soul.

I have used every fictional tool I know. Sometimes, *The Red Ribbon* reads like memoir, but more often it crosses into the territory of fiction. Of course, I had to create the dialog.

Occasionally, I stumbled onto the perfect words. For instance, when my dad calls me "Nance" and "Girlie" in "The Beaches," and in "The Old Spaniel," he sounds so real to me that it is as though he is alive again for a few moments. And I get teary. My goal was to capture the truth, and although I often invent the specifics, I have captured my heart's truth, which is what I value most.

The Red Ribbon is true.

The summer sky of my youth was Montana blue. Its wide expanse like a magnificent tent offered me beauty and usually safety. But on certain afternoons in July and August, meadowlarks stopped their melodies, killdeer hurried back to their nests made of stones, and long-legged jackrabbits fled into their burrows. Thunder rumbled; lightning flashed; the western sky grew dark. A gray wash began in the distant Beartooth Mountains and soon colored my world as though a giant brush were painting the sky with diluted black.

By mid-afternoon, the oppressive heat would rise into the high nineties, sometimes even over a hundred, and set off palpable anxiety in me. The afternoon storms rarely delivered a refreshing rain. The wind stirred up sandy grit that blew on my tanned face and against my bare arms and legs; a few sparse drops fell, but that was all. The local weatherman reported again on the black-and-white TV news at dinnertime, "No appreciable rain for Billings and its vicinity." The banks of the wide Yellowstone River, the fields of alfalfa, and acres of feed corn nearby were dry as tumbleweed.

Early each summer, my father took me aside and said "Nance, soon as it looks like a storm, get yourself home." He settled his blue eyes on mine, "I mean it. Don't get stuck at your

friend Susie's. Your mother will worry if you're not home."
Neither of us wanted to worry my mother.

So when the sky to the west threatened rain, I ran home
closing the screen door carefully behind me while other children in my neighborhood let their screen doors slam. "I'm
home," I called out to my mother. And without being told, I
began the task of moving from room to room, closing windows.

Almost once a summer, a serious storm arrived; thunder
and lightning announced the onslaught of torrential rain,
pounding hail. Thumb-sized slugs of ice caused real damage—
denting our car, bruising the cedar siding on the west wall of
our house, and breaking many of the small panes of glass in
our windows. The cruel hail battered our garden, ruining our
tomatoes and strawberries, scattering their red flesh onto the
dusty pale earth.

One summer during a bad storm, a child running across
Pioneer Park tripped into a gully and was pummeled by hail to
unconsciousness. My mother read me the news story and
showed me the photos published on the front page of *The
Billings Gazette*. She said, "That could have been you." Tugging
at my shirt, she asked, "And then how would I have felt?" I
didn't plan to come home via Pioneer Park or fall down and
get banged up, but I heard her. I understood. *Storms arrived;
danger came with them.*

During those rare bad storms, we three with our family's
springer spaniel sat in the dim light of the basement wondering out loud when the power would fail. My dad and I took
turns during the lulls in the storm to assess the glass damage.
"Girlie, you go this time," he would say, and I would speed up
the stairs to investigate. Our family measured the intensity of
the storms by the number of windowpanes we lost—eleven
wasn't bad; twenty-seven was our worst.

Home insurance paid for materials and labor to repair our modest house, but most summers, my parents delayed the replacement of the siding. My mother, who managed the budget, reasoned that a little money could be made if my father patched the holes and painted the clapboards. "It'll just happen again next summer," she reasoned. "We'll wait." By doing temporary repairs, my father could create a windfall income while he was on summer vacation from teaching. He attempted the repairs atop an aluminum ladder that trembled; it made me nervous. I wondered that my mother didn't see how inexpert he was, two stories up in the air.

I acted as my dad's assistant, and we talked as he worked. "I get as much paint on the ground as I do on the siding," he joked as he dripped Sagebrush Green in random circles on the concrete walkway. "Careful, Dad," I said each time I handed up a brush or a can of paint.

In 1959, the August I turned sixteen, the Hebgen Lake Earthquake in Yellowstone Park caused a landslide that claimed the lives of twenty-eight, some of them campers caught in their tents asleep; the earthquake sundered roads and ripped the forest floor apart. Although my hometown was one hundred and fifty miles northeast of the epicenter, my family was awakened late at night, the walls of our house in Billings shaking. "Get under a doorway," my father shouted at me. And so we stood, my parents in the doorway of their bedroom, me in mine, listening to fragile objects fall and break all around the house until the initial shocks of the quake subsided. "That sure was something," my dad said.

One summer afternoon when I was in high school, I experienced my first tornado. I stood on our upper patio with a view of the western sky. Beyond our lilac hedges, beyond the neighbors' backyards and farmers' fields of cornstalks and wheat, I caught sight of the horizon. I had seen the curtain of sky blackened with storm clouds before, but now for the first time I viewed long black threads morphing into swirling funnels, watched them reaching down grazing the land.

"Come downstairs," my mother shouted at me from the basement. And when I didn't show up, I heard her yell, "Go get her, John."

My father came to the back door. "Nance, you've got to come in." But now, I was older. I said, "Dad, you're going to want to see this." And for a few minutes, we stood side by side, the wind whipping our cotton clothes as we watched classic funnels grow bigger and bigger, closer and closer. I was mesmerized, fascinated, frozen. My dad took me by the wrist and pulled me inside the house; behind us, the screen slapped shut.

As a girl, I learned that my Montana sky was wide and beautiful. Some summer afternoons, dangerous storms came. They came right out of the blue.

PART I

ARCS AND SPARKS

Nancy, wake up," Sarah says shaking me by the shoulder. "Get out of bed."

Her somber tone catches my attention. In one motion, I sit up on the guest room's twin mattress, causing a quilt to fall away from my thin cotton gown. I hold up the face of my watch to the narrow slit of light streaming in from the upstairs hallway. It's three o'clock in the morning. Sarah is waking me at three in the morning.

"Get up. Get dressed as fast as you can," Sarah, my husband's older sister, says and she closes the door. With only the light of the moon, I fumble in my overnight bag and search for underpants and a bra. I'm thinking, *I'm tired and want to go back to bed.* To slip into my jeans, I lean against a wall to avoid stumbling. Even as I pull a T-shirt over my head, I'm thinking, *What's happened? Are Geoff and the boys safe?*

I haul on a sweatshirt; even a July night is chilly in Maine. As I kneel on the new-smelling carpeting to lace up my sneakers, my fingers feel thick.

In the bathroom, I splash water on my face and rake through my mouth with my toothbrush not taking time for toothpaste. I position myself outside Sarah and Marshall's closed bedroom door waiting, listening. I hear a few words: "nurse . . . emergency room . . . York Hospital." I tilt my head to hear better. More words: "lightning . . . accident . . . not good."

Marshall, my brother-in-law, emerges from the bedroom squinting away sleep. He puts on his wire-rimmed glasses. "Ready?" he asks me avoiding eye contact.

"Yes, ready," I say although I'm not sure for what.

As we three stand together on the second floor landing, Sarah says, "A nurse from York Hospital called." As we race down the steep stairway, she calls out, "Geoff and Teddy have been in an accident." Geoff, my husband. Teddy, my twenty-year-old son.

As the screen door slams behind us, I try to process the information. I am jumping ahead of myself, putting words together, enough words to know I wish to go backward in time. I want to retrace my steps, to cover myself in the white gauze of my nightgown and to burrow under the safety of the quilt; I want to escape back in time before three o'clock in the morning of July 24, 1994.

My body is tossed across the backseat of the Ford Explorer as Marshall makes a sharp left turn onto Route 77. As we pass under the blinking light near Cape Elizabeth's town hall, I ask, "What else did the nurse say?"

I count ten seconds as Marshall and Sarah each wait for the other to answer. Sarah says deliberately, "The nurse said, 'Get to the hospital as fast as you can.'"

I take in that news, but can't keep from asking, "What else?"

"She said they were hit by lightning."

"Oh, God," I say. Solemn silence follows.

As Marshall takes the shortcut to avoid Crescent Beach, as Fowler Road winds and dips, I lift myself out of my body. No longer dressed in the pastels of summer, no longer inside flesh at all, I watch the woman who sits in the blackness of the back-seat. I observe her with compassion and watch the shadow of her head bow in silent prayer.

Please, I hear her beg God. *Please, don't let it be both of them.*

I HAD DRIVEN up to Cape Elizabeth, Maine, from Deer-field, New Hampshire, because I needed Sarah's loving support; she was my husband's older sister but also my friend. After twenty-six years of marriage, Geoff and I were estranged and yes, separated. Ostensibly, I went to help Sarah and Marshall unpack boxes and settle into their summer home, but I knew I was going for their support and company.

I wasn't sure what direction my life was taking. Day by day, I felt like I was camping out.

Marshall spent his time unpacking books and wine. Sarah and I worked side by side pulling out storm windows, washing the multiple panes and inserting screens. With each exchange, we felt the fleeting warmth of summer sun on our faces and hands; we inhaled the sea air and sensed the seasons of our lives shift.

For dinner, we three went to Joe's Boathouse in South Portland, a marina-restaurant with an excellent view of Casco Bay. On the porch waiting among tourists, we toasted their new home with a crisp Pinot Grigio. For starters, we shared garlicky steamed mussels and for entrées, shellfish and pasta. Over coffee, we concluded that the Maine coast was a place of peace and perfection.

It was a beautiful day—no rain, no thunder, no lightning.

WHEN MARSHALL HALTS the Explorer at the tollgate near the Maine Mall, none of us can find two quarters so a frustrated attendant waves us on. On the straightaway of the Maine Turnpike, I witness the SUV's speedometer jiggle between 90 and 95. But my body wearies of sitting on the edge of my seat and holding onto Sarah's headrest for balance. Barely aware of time and place, I watch the traffic signs as they whiz past like shaky ghosts in the extra black of the night.

"How much farther is it?" Sarah asks.

"I don't know," Marshall answers. He is the kind of man who always knows. But now, he doesn't.

"Careful," Sarah says twice—first as we pass the exit at Biddeford and then at Wells. I think I can read her mind. She is thinking we needn't kill ourselves racing to the hospital if Geoff and Teddy are already dead.

As a social worker, I know the drill. You don't tell relatives their loved ones have died. Not until they arrive at the hospital. Tell them there's been an accident. Tell them their relative—father, mother, husband, wife, child, is seriously, even critically injured. But wait, wait with the news of death.

My mind analyzes the data—it is three o'clock in the morning, my husband and son have been in an accident, and it is pitch dark on the coast of Maine. Can they still be alive?

I close my eyes and pray. "Please, God," I ask. "Geoff would want Teddy to live. If he had a choice, he would choose Teddy." And I add, "If it were me, I would choose to die." Then I am afraid. I think, *What if God hears me and is repulsed by my thoughts, my prayers? What if I am praying for the wrong thing?* So I begin the mantra, *Please, God, your will. Let it be your will.*

Absently, I begin patting and stroking the velvety upholstery of the backseat. It reminds me of hugging and kissing Teddy goodbye as he loaded the kayaks; I feel him warm in my arms.

And on the phone with Geoff, I said, "I can't keep up with

the raspberries. Help yourself when you come to cut the grass."
I hope he knew those were words of conciliation. After the
images of kayaks and black water, I see arcs and sparks of
lightning and love. And then nothing. The Explorer is following blue-and-white rectangular
signs to York Hospital via York Beach. When it turns a corner,
I can see the York amusement park. How strange the Ferris
wheel looks spinning like an enormous roulette wheel as we
roll by. I want to be lucky tonight, but I am afraid to pray for
luck. Someone is going to be unlucky, and I don't want to be
the one to tilt the odds.

Outside York Hospital, when the SUV brakes, I stumble
out; my legs break into a run, but inside the vacuum of the
emergency room doorways, they slow down. I walk through
the ER entrance and head for the admitting desk.

Joanna, a friend and colleague, stops me. I lean down to
receive her embrace; our cheeks touch, and I feel her tears.
Joanna is petite so I must bend myself in two. "Geoff's dead,"
she whispers into my ear. Then she hurries to add, "But Teddy
is alive."

"Geoff's dead?" I ask, and Joanna hugs me tight. Sarah approaches us, and I tell her, "Geoff is dead." It comes out more
question than statement. "I'm sorry," I tell Sarah. Geoff is her
younger brother.

Joanna tugs at the sleeve of my sweatshirt. "Go say goodbye to Geoff," she points me toward a nurse who leads me
down a labyrinth of hallways. I hurry to keep up, but I have
trouble moving my legs because inside my head a voice is
screaming, *This can't be true.* The voice, my voice is repeating,
Geoff can't be dead. This must be a mistake. He can't be dead.

The nurse motions me into a small sterile room. I step inside.
Geoff's body lies on a gurney draped in a white sheet. Only his
head is exposed. I pause several steps from the gurney. *Kiss him*

goodbye, my mind tells my lips. *You can do this.* I approach him; his face is badly swollen. He doesn't look like himself at all. *You must do this, and then you can go to Teddy.*

I lean toward his face, I close my eyes and my lips kiss his cheek; it is cool.

The nurse waits for me at the doorway where Joanna says to me, "You need to sign the forms for an autopsy." I feel my face frown in confusion; my head shakes no, but she says, "The nurse needs your signature so Geoff's body can be taken to the morgue." In spite of my doubts, I do what she asks. I must sign my name.

As I follow the nurse out of the emergency room, across the hallway, and into the ICU, Joanna follows as far as the ICU station. When the nurse with the power of life and death draws back a curtain, I see Teddy, my Teddy, lying on a hospital bed, a bed cranked upward as far as it will go. Medical apparatus are crowded around him.

Teddy's face is obscured by the mouthpiece of a ventilator. And he's pale, but his hair, dark and curly, is reassuring. His shoulders are broad like his father's. *But his eyes, I tell myself, his eyes under closed lids, the eyes I can't see, are like mine not his dad's. Not hazel and gone. But blue, alive.*

I sit down in a plastic chair and reach out to hold Teddy's hand. I hold it carefully; it is warm. At first, my attention is absorbed by his heartbeat beeping and scrolling on the heart monitor's screen. When its alarm goes off, I stand and cry out for a nurse. One comes. She checks Teddy and waves a practiced hand at me. Her gesture says my son is all right; his heart is beating. The other machine, the one responsible for Teddy's breathing makes *whoosh*-like noises. I am so thankful for these two machines.

I sit and reposition my hand. I close my eyes and remember the last time holding Teddy's hand seemed so critical. I had walked him the few blocks from our big white house on Airport Hill to Teague Park Elementary School. That fall day in Caribou, Maine, was cool; the air was dry. We took turns clasping each other's hands, but as our fingers reached out in practiced ritual, I knew our lives were changing forever. On the way home, returning down the dusty gravel road after I had delivered him to kindergarten, I knew my life as a woman and as a mother had plunged into a new season. I saw a stand of Japanese lanterns against a neighbor's fence; the orange air-filled bells were delicate, their veins visible in the sunlight; they hung from slender, painful stems. Now, here I was holding his hand again.

Sometime later, a nurse slides in beside me. I'm startled and jam my chair against the hospital bed. Smiling down at me, she taps the IV bag, follows the tubing with her fingertips to Teddy's tan, muscular arm. She seems satisfied.

I drift. Minutes, hours later, I'm unsure when, Sarah kisses my cheek. She asks, "Would you like me to sit with him? You need a break?"

"No," I say. "I can't leave him."

"We'll need to call the family," she says. "Not now. But in the morning."

"Not now," I say. "Later." And I see concern on her face. She disappears.

I'M NOT SURE for how long I sit and watch the heart monitor, listen to the ventilator. Perhaps I drift off, but sometime near sunrise, my eyes shift from the magic machines to a nurse in blue scrubs. I study her as she takes note of Teddy's vital signs and records them on his chart. With all my impaired ability, I struggle to look inside her eyes to see what she sees in Teddy's future. Yes, I can tell she believes that this young life will continue. And I begin to have hope that Teddy is going to make it.

AROUND EIGHT O'CLOCK in the morning, Simon, Teddy's older brother, arrives with his wife, Emily, from Lake George, all the way from New York State, a long ride for them. My exhausted and worried older son relieves me, taking up my post; he holds Teddy's hand as lovingly as I have.

Outside the curtains, next to the patients' charts, an ICU nurse offers me tea and hands me tissues. Her kindness melts all my resolve to keep control of my emotions. I weep.

According to Simon, he learned about the lightning accident in much the same way I did. Both of us were away from our homes so the staff at York Hospital had difficulty locating us. The accident occurred on July 23 in the middle of the afternoon, but we were not notified until a good twelve hours later.

PERHAPS A SUBTLE vibration in the universe awakens Simon or more likely the rumble of a boat's engine out on Lake George disturbs his sleep. A July moon shines down through the skylight of the bunk house. He studies his watch. It is 3:00 a.m. He and Emily are at his in-laws' place. Emily, his wife of two years, her auburn hair spread out on the pillow beside him, is sleeping soundly. No reason to wake her. He eases out of the bed and pulls on a navy T-shirt with the faded logo of Outward Bound—To Strive, To Serve, and Not to Yield.

It is unlike Simon to wake during the night. Maybe there was a noise out on the lake; sound travels across the water. Or maybe he drank an extra beer. Either way, now he needs to climb the stone steps from the bunkhouse to the main house. The camp's one big shortcoming is its single bathroom. But the family has a sense of pride and solidarity around the inconvenience. After all, it's a camp; it's supposed to be rustic—one bathroom, no TV, no phone.

Simon likes the privacy of the bunkhouse, but even he who loves backpacking and camping misses a bathroom at three in the morning. He walks to the sliding door that opens not far from the dock. He thinks, *Much easier to just piss off the dock.*

Simon stands on the dock releasing a healthy stream into the bay. He is still in the half-asleep world one can maintain when there are no interruptions. He is looking forward to climbing back in bed with Emily and sleeping late on Sunday.

But then, the blare of a boat's insistent horn breaks the quiet. A twenty-four-foot cabin cruiser with a great array of lights comes charging into the private bay, barreling toward the dock. The boat's bright lights shine on Simon. His first sleepy thought is that it must be against the law to urinate in Lake George. This must be the police coming to arrest him. But such thoughts are nonsense. He is suddenly awake, alarmed, angry. But studying the boat, Simon quickly recognizes it as the *Lazy Daisy*; the man at the helm is Emily's Uncle Burt. When Burt cuts the engine, Simon calls out, "What's wrong?!"

"Hold on." Burt orders. "Tie her up." Simon rushes forward to catch the line. As Burt climbs off the boat, he asks, "Where's Emily? I need to talk to you both."

Emily appears at the door of the bunkhouse in a purple nightshirt; she is pulling on her jeans. Burt motions to Simon and to Emily, "Both of you need to get something warm on. It's freezin' out on the lake, and you've got to come with me."

As Simon dives into the bunkhouse, Burt gestures for Emily to wait by the door. He speaks quietly. "Your mother called," he says. "It's bad news. There's been an accident." He nods toward Simon. "His father and his brother."

"How bad?" Emily asks. Burt shakes his head. He doesn't know. "Where?" she asks.

"In Maine. You're going to have to drive to York, Maine, tonight. To the hospital there."

THE DAY HAD been idyllic—in the high eighties but with a breeze. Simon took a morning hike along paths near the water's edge but then struck out into the old growth of the woods. Charlie, his beagle, bayed and barked at squirrels, chased them up tree trunks. When Simon returned, he finished several small repairs from a long list his father-in-law keeps on the bulletin board in the kitchen. The traditional Adirondack house of stone and cedar always needs maintenance.

In the afternoon, Simon and Emily had taken the Boston Whaler across the lake to a little known sandy beach. Under a cloudless sky, they went swimming in almost-warm water, sunbathed on the boat. Then, they went back to the camp and made dinner—steak and salad with Vermont's Magic Hat beer. After dinner, they listened to records and played Monopoly; he won. They went to bed early. It was both strange and exciting to be away from their University of Vermont graduate school housing in Burlington and to be at the camp alone.

ONCE EMILY AND Uncle Burt join Simon in the dim light of the bunkhouse, she relays the news to Simon. "My mom called Uncle Burt," she says. "Your dad and Teddy are hurt, some kind of accident." She hugs Simon. "I'm so sorry," she whispers into his ear.

Burt says, "They were out boating. Some kind of storm came up."

"How bad are they?" Simon asks. Burt shakes his head; he doesn't know.

Despite his shock, Simon peppers Burt with more questions, but Burt isn't able to add much. He finally has to say, "I don't know what more to tell you. I'm sorry. Sis just said for you to get to the hospital in Maine."

Emily packs the little bit they brought to the camp—their shorts, T-shirts, and swimsuits. Her birth control pills. Not much. Simon feels paralyzed, but he grabs Charlie's leash and kibble. Charlie barks until he is carried aboard.

When their canvas bags are stowed inside the boat's cabin, when the lines are loosed, Burt flips on the engine, and the boat hums out of the cove. The night is black; dense clouds have smothered the stars and moon. Simon is shocked that the usual landmarks are missing; even the shadowy shoreline disappears as the cabin cruiser picks up speed to streak over the giant lake.

"Go on inside," Burt says to Simon slapping the young man's shoulder. "No use for us both to freeze."

But inside the cramped space below, the combination of dog smell and anxiety combine to make Simon nauseous.

"Sorry, I'm going up top," he says to Emily. He pats Charlie's head; the dog is lying on the V-berth whining. "Shush," Simon says. "You're okay." He strokes the tan-and-black dog's coarse fur coat. "You're okay. We're all okay." He climbs up the ladder tasting tears in his mouth.

Standing beside Burt, Simon endures the endless ride across Lake George. Both men are silent. Part way, Simon walks to the stern prepared to vomit; he retches and can smell a whiff of his supper—onions and beer. But nothing comes up.

The ride across Lake George is painful for Simon; he keeps feeling that he is going to vomit. With the cold and the high waves, crossing Lake George is like crossing an ocean.

When Simon and Emily arrive at Bolton's Landing, she is the one who finds their car in the marina's parking lot. It is all so surreal. Simon's father is so vital. His little brother, Teddy, is not little. Twenty. The two most important men in his life.

Simon drives. Too fast. Near Woodstock, a Vermont state trooper pulls them over. "What's the rush?" he asks. When their story tumbles out, he waves them on. He both cautions them, "Careful" and wishes them "Good luck!"

Near Concord, New Hampshire, Emily offers to drive. Simon sits in the passenger seat with Charlie, compact and muscular, on his lap. The dog's body heat warms Simon, helps protect him from his worst fears. Simon holds onto Charlie; Emily drives. According to the map, with no traffic on the roads, they should arrive at York Hospital at about 8:00 a.m.

t h r e e

THE CLIPPINGS

The following excerpts from newspaper articles are provided here as documentation of the lightning accident; the clippings are from the *Portsmouth Herald, The Boston Globe, USA Today, The Manchester Union Leader* and *the New York Times.* They are placed in chronological order:

PORTSMOUTH HERALD SUNDAY

Sunday, July 24, 1994, $1.25 Single Copy

LIGHTNING BOLT STRIKES FORT FOSTER
BYSTANDERS TRY TO SAVE KAYAKERS

KITTERY—Lightning strike victims' names
are being withheld until relatives can be notified.

———

At Fort Foster, police interviewed shaken witnesses. "It was terrible," said Brian Bruce, one of a dozen picnickers who worked in the downpour and hail to try to restore the victims' heartbeats. "One still had no pulse when the ambulance arrived."

Brian was picking up a croquet set only about 10 yards away from the bunker when he saw a white flash and heard thunder almost simultaneously. He was knocked down by the bolt and got up in time to see a man, who appeared to be holding the railing on the top of the bunker, fall down. Like the other rescuers who helped the victims, Bruce encountered a powerful burning smell and blood. When he began CPR, the breaths he took in tasted of charcoal. . . .

THE BOSTON GLOBE
JULY 25, 1994

KAYAKER DIES AFTER LIGHTNING STRIKE

KITTERY, Maine—Psychologist died and his son remained hospitalized yesterday after they were struck by lightning. Kittery Police Chief, Robert Magnuson, said Geoffrey Green, 48, of Deerfield, New Hampshire, died at 3:50 a.m. at York Hospital. Green's son, Theodore, 20, remained in the intensive care unit.

USA TODAY
TUESDAY JULY 26, 1994

NEWS FROM EVERY STATE

MAINE...KITTERY—Kayakers did the right thing by getting off the water and taking shelter in a World War I–era bunker when a storm arose, officials said. However, lightning struck the bunker, killing Geoffrey Green, 48.

THE UNION LEADER, Manchester, N.H.—

Wednesday, July 27, 1994

KITTERY POINT LIGHTNING SURVIVOR
MOVED OUT OF ICU

KITTERY, Maine—Survivor of the lightning strike at Fort Foster this past weekend has been moved out of intensive care. Theodore Green, 20, of Deerfield, N.H. is listed in satisfactory condition at York Hospital. Green's father, Geoffrey, was killed as a result of the lightning strike. Father and son were kayaking on Kittery Bay when they sought shelter from a sudden afternoon thunderstorm in a gun bunker at Fort Foster. Lightning struck. . . .

———

NEW YORK TIMES OBITUARIES

SUNDAY, AUGUST 7, 1994

DEATHS:

GREEN—Geoffrey Chaucer, 48, died suddenly and tragically in York, Maine on July 24, 1994. Husband of Nancy Bills Green, father of Simon Green and Theodore Green, son . . ., brother . . ., friend . . ., psychologist. . . . He will be greatly missed.

f o u r

THE PIZZA BOX

I want to tell you something, Mom," Teddy says. We've finished a pepperoni pizza from the Deerfield Country Store. He stacks our dirty plates in the middle of the kitchen table. I carry them to the sink and drop paper napkins smeared with tomato sauce into the trash. Neither of us has been doing much cooking since the lightning accident in July; now it's mid-November, and discarded take-out pizza boxes are piling up in the garage.

Teddy and I don't always have dinner together. Although we live in the same house, our daily lives are often parallel. He's probably tired of my asking about his medical appointments. I cringe when I think of how many times I've asked, "What does your doctor say?" He always answers, "I'm making satisfactory progress, Mom." And then I ask, "And you like your therapist?" And he says, "Yes, I do."

Teddy and I rarely phone his brother, Simon, who has his wife, Emily, to comfort him, and for company, he has her family, a family untouched by tragedy. We three survivors of the lightning strike love each other, but right now, we barely know what to say to one another. And often, contact with each other causes us fresh pain, pain we all want to avoid.

Honestly, I'm a mess. My therapist's diagnosis is "complicated grief." She says grief takes longer when your relationship has been in turmoil. My psychiatrist has prescribed Prozac for depression, Ativan for anxiety, and Ambien for insomnia. I'm only able to fall asleep if I leave both bedside lamps on. I learned from the accident that it's when lights are turned off and you go to sleep that tragedy happens. I know I'm being irrational, but I don't seem to be able to help myself.

Two weeks after Geoff's death, I returned to Concord Regional Hospital to an internship in hospital social work. I'm filling in for a social worker on maternity leave. Four days a week, I carefully drive the thirty minutes to Concord Hospital. Now, I do everything carefully; my sons don't deserve to lose another parent. Being busy helps. Being out of the house ought to help. But I never know when something—often a song on the radio, will ambush me. I try to anticipate the experiences that will overwhelm me, but I'm often wrong. I startle, even yelp, at sudden, unexpected noises.

Almost everyone at the hospital knows about the lightning accident; the coverage was extensive in all the local papers. I know people want to be kind, but in the middle of my work day, I don't want to be reminded that I'm a widow. Or that I almost lost a son. I pray, *Oh, God, just don't let me cry.* I focus on my patients—look them in the eye and listen to them. Get them what they will need when they go home from the hospital. I don't even mind the paperwork. I know I need a job to do, a role to fill, something meaningful, but I don't want any life or death responsibility for others, just a long list of tasks that will crowd out my awareness that my life and my sons' lives will never be the same. Geoff is dead.

I dread returning home to rooms so evocative that they remind me of the happy and the sad; both make me weep. At the end of the day, I often linger in the social workers' break room. "Don't be too nice to me," I tell Debby and Francine who are training me. But they never let me leave without hugs.

I worry about Teddy, whose nursery school teacher, the lovable if flamboyant Auntie Margaret, said she could talk to him as though he were an adult. My precocious boy! Is he going to be able to return to college? After all, he's still having problems with his balance, memory, and concentration. How will my beautiful son with his head of dark curly hair, my boy who at fourteen trailed behind the veterinarian at the horse barn, support himself? Will he ever go kayaking again? Does he even want to? Will he be safe skiing? Biking? Is anything safe?

"Mom?" Teddy asks.

We stand in the kitchen, me with a dish towel over my shoulder in the same way I used to drape a diaper in case Baby Teddy or Baby Simon spit up.

"I've decided to go back to Baltimore, back to school."

I assume he has talked this over with his therapist, the one he likes. "Good," I say. "You feel ready for that?"

"Yeah," he says. "It's worth a try. How will I know otherwise?"

"So next semester?" I ask. "In January?"

"Well, no," he says. "Now."

"Oh," I say. "So after Thanksgiving?"

"Actually," Teddy says, "I'm planning on going next week."

He fills in the details—he will take his belongings in his Chevy truck, stay with friends, and search for an apartment. Aslan, his Golden Retriever puppy, named for the lion in C. S. Lewis' Narnia tales, will go with him. I can't forget that Lewis created Aslan as the symbol of God. *God go with you, my son,* I think.

"Oh," I say. I can tell Teddy has been thinking about leaving for weeks. My chest hurts, but my role is clear. He is twenty years old. Almost twenty-one. He has a reasonable plan. He deserves my full support. I must not express my fears, fears so close to his own.

"Oh," I say. "Well, okay." I pick up the grease-stained pizza box and toss it out the back door into the garage and onto the pile of other take-out boxes.

f i v e

THE EMPTYING
AND FILLING OF
THE DRAWER

The Christmas after Geoff's death, I visit my son, Teddy, in Baltimore. We say goodnight. As I close the door of his spare room, I walk to the twin bed and unzip my suitcase. I pull out a flannel nightgown and my toothbrush. Then I see it. On a table. Teddy's assemblage. Created in my son's darkest moments in the months after his father's death, the base of his sculpture is the drawer of his childhood desk; its insides are his grief.

After a streak of lightning killed his father, the building of the sculpture grew into Teddy's salvation, his instinct converting pain, anger, and fear into art. First, Teddy filled the drawer, the void, with the turntable of an old record player; he broke one of his Dad's favorite records, David Mallett's *Inches and Miles*, in quarters over it.

The following day, I watched as Teddy took his lacrosse stick, something he was proud of, and cracked it in two. He thrust the splintered stick into the drawer; the mesh of the basket quivered in the airspace above the brittle black plastic of the record.

Later, I witnessed Teddy take one of his father's running shoes, pull the laces out of the eyelets, bend the tongue forward and place the sole carefully in the exact crosshairs of the shallow drawer. The effect was that a phantom racer would return at night and run life's marathon again.

Near the end of Teddy's creative burst, he took his jeans and his windbreaker, upended the pockets, and let lint and sand, his private accumulations of life's dust, sift down on the drawer-sized grave. And with a bare forefinger, he drew in the date of his father's death: 7-24-94.

As I watched Teddy create his sculpture, I was filled with wonder at how art allows us to survive.

The filling of Teddy's drawer seemed both careful and random, symbolic and meaningless. One day, he brought a horseshoe home from the barn, turned it upside down, and placed it so that luck ran out from every angle. Another day, looking like a child, as thoroughly regressed as I was, he cradled and nuzzled the family of teddy bears he had loved all his life and gave up the button nose of his first teddy bear. It had been worn off with play and saved to be restored, but he sacrificed it to the sculpture. In one of the last acts of a young artist, he tucked the breathless nose in a corner of the drawer.

Then Teddy, artist and son, completed his creative effort by pouring black enamel over all the chosen representations of his young grief. After the ooze dried like crude oil over a seabird, and only with his blessing, I opened a milkweed pod and scattered the white silk and seeds in a hopeful streak over the drawer's contents.

Art sustains us.

AFTER BRUSHING MY teeth, I close the door of the guest room. Murmur a prayer.

s i x

A HEAD OF LETTUCE

n January of 1995, I'm employed at Concord Regional Hospital in New Hampshire. One noontime as I slide my red plastic tray onto one of cafeteria's tables, my new friend, Maxine, says, "Don't let me forget. I've got something for you."

"Okay," I say and sit down at the large round table full of noisy females. Maxine is finishing an off-color joke, and I see a hospital administrator at a nearby table frown. Now Maxine is laughing and turning to smile at me. She and I are the only social workers on staff with master's degrees and the only single women at the table.

I still have reservations about my new job as a member of a treatment team on a locked psychiatric floor; it's not what I wanted but what was available. The work is demanding, but these foolish and often raucous lunches with Maxine and my other social work friends are a great break from working with patients struggling with serious mental illness. Maxine, a family therapist, works on the outpatient wing. A few years my senior, she has adopted me as her new project.

"Listen," she says to the others. "Nancy doesn't know it, but she's going to meet the man of her dreams this weekend." They laugh. I envy my friends their husbands, their children, their homes tucked in central New Hampshire villages near Concord.

I must drive the now bleak and icy back country roads to my house in north Deerfield.

After work, Mr. Puss, my aging white and orange cat, will come running through the hoary grasses and reeds of my field to welcome me home to our otherwise empty Cape. I'm determined not to spend the winter out in the lonely countryside. A former patient of mine, a mother of two children, has lost her home to a fire. I've offered her my house for the winter, a gift to us both. I plan to rent a condo in Concord.

Maxine teases me. "You're getting too skinny. No man is going to be interested in you if you lose any more weight. Come on." And so we get up and choose the ice cream flavor of the day, maple walnut. It was Geoff's favorite. I can feel my eyes threaten to water. Between masterful licks of ice cream, Maxine hands me a newsletter. "It's not a singles' dating club," she says. "It's an activity club."

"Sure," I say and hand it right back. "I'm not ready."

"You're not ready?!" Maxine asks with exaggerated drama. "Geoff's dead," she says. "But in case you didn't notice, you're not."

"Shhh," I say and look around the cafeteria, but it's mostly empty. No one is listening. Before we leave, she spreads the newsletter out on the tabletop and points to a notice marked with yellow highlighter.

"This is the meeting you should go to," Maxine says. "There will be guys there." I read the announcement: men and women with an interest in joining the Concord Area Singles Activity Club are invited to a planning session on Friday night at 7:00 p.m. at the Concord Tennis Club. "You and I can go out for a quick bite after work," she says. "I'll even come with you if you want me to." She grins at me. This is a threat. If she accompanies me, she'll play Jewish matchmaker, and it will be oh so embarrassing.

"No," I blurt out. "I can go by myself."

"You'll be all right," Maxine says. "Just pretend you're going to the grocery store. You're in a rush. You need a head of lettuce." She adds hand gestures to her expressive voice. "Just reach out and pick one."

"I don't know," I say.

"I do. I know you'll be fine," Maxine says. "Just smile. You know how to smile. Don't you?" I nod. Then, she pleads, "Promise me you'll go."

"Okay," I say, "I promise."

"No more bereavement groups for you," she says. "It's time you reenter the world of the living."

So I FIND my courage and show up at the planning meeting of the Concord Area Singles Activity Club. I pay the nominal fee of $10 to join, fill out a name tag with a red marker, and sit down at the table. Maxine is right. I can do this.

Introductions begin. Most of the men and the few women present are board members and chairmen of committees. I study the people seated around the large oval table. As the men introduce themselves, I listen to what they do, examine their faces, and try to imagine myself on a date with one of them. The only man I'm attracted to, a high school history teacher, has a girlfriend, the woman sitting next to him patting his arm. Nope. It's a washout.

The moderator asks for ideas. Someone looks at me, and I say I would like to go cross-country skiing. Others would too. Then, the door opens and a latecomer arrives with no apology. The tall and not-bad-looking man takes off a parka and throws it with some panache across an empty table. I catch his eye, and he pulls a chair up next to me. We smile. He says his name is Jules. He asks, "Did I miss anything?"

And I say with studied nonchalance, "Not much."

"What do you like to do?" he asks.

I whisper, "Cross-country ski. Downhill, too."

"Sailing?" he asks.

"Yes," I say surprising myself with my genuine enthusiasm.

He takes a photo of his sailboat out of his wallet and shows it to me. Our hands touch. I have selected my head of lettuce.

A white pickup hit young Mr. Puss
a glancing blow, and he
took to ground the way cats do.
He was missing and missed.

I thought that was that,
but Mr. Puss came home,
wary though. I'd kneel down beside
him, put my head under the old
railroad bench we used as an
end table. (We were furniture poor.)

I'd say kind, loving words and
he'd pretend he wasn't listening.
He liked me a little after that.
He was lean, proud, mightily independent.

My favorite thing at the end of a day
was to watch him running across the meadow
toward the noise of my car.
He'd come leaping through the tall
grass for all the world like
a Russian dancer dressed in white tights.

Then he'd stop short just in time
to look at my car, the flowers, a tree,
to look at everything but me
and rub against my legs purring.
He lived the longest of all the
Boot Hill cats. An old man, his rear legs
gave out. He climbed the couch
dragging himself up by his "arms."

Jules, my boyfriend, said,
"You should put him down."
"But he's so brave. I can't."
"It's easy." he said. "Humane."

And the kind vet did it well.
Mr. Puss was seventeen . . . and then he wasn't.

On a clear summer day in 1995, I sit across from Teddy in the living room of his apartment on the Maryland Shore. I've waited for months to ask him a question, postponed it until he found a job he liked and began dating a nurse regularly. I sigh and ask him, "What do you remember about the accident?"

Teddy stares out a window that has a partial view of open ocean. He is silent for several seconds. "The last thing I remember is lunch," he answers, "lunch with Dad on a little island in Portsmouth Bay. That's the last thing—tuna fish sandwiches and potato chips."

"And a Mountain Dew, I bet."

"Yeah, a Mountain Dew."

I ask, "What about kayaking after lunch or the storm?" I watch his face, "Or anything about Fort Foster or the bunker?" He shakes his head. And I think, *No memory of the sudden dark clouds, the boom of thunder. Not the rush to get off the water or the beaching of the kayaks. Not the pelting rain, the hail. Not running across the park or the race up the concrete steps to a WWI bunker.*

"Too many questions?" I ask although they have all been inside my head.

"No. No, Mom, it's actually good to talk about it." I sigh. *So much he doesn't remember. Not the streak of lightning zooming across the summer afternoon sky, not the lightning bolt exploding into the steel beams of the bunker. So much he doesn't ever need to know.*

I smile at my son who is leaning back in a comfortable chair with his feet on an ottoman. "You look so well," I say. Teddy smiles indulgently. I reassure myself, *No memory of a sizzle entering the back of his head and exiting above his sneakers. No memory of sirens screaming around fallen tree limbs and live power lines. And blessedly no memory of himself and his father lying only feet apart on a cracked concrete floor.*

"So," I say, "just lunch? And then? What next?"

"The memorial service."

"Oh, do you remember the service?"

"No," Teddy answers. "Nothing about the service itself. It's like I just wake up in the receiving line. I remember Simon patting my shoulder." And I remember my two sons standing side by side shaking the hands of hundreds of mourners.

"Anything else?" I ask. "Anything after you got transferred out of the ICU? Do you remember any visitors?" Teddy shakes his head. "What about the brothers who were at the park having a picnic who gave you CPR?" *For twenty-five critical minutes.* "Do you remember them? Or the ambulance team from South Berwick?" The men were so happy to see him alive. And on the Med/Surg Floor, my son had seemed awake, aware.

"No, I don't remember." Teddy frowns and shakes his head. But then he holds a hand to his mouth. "In the hospital, I do remember something." He grimaces. "Like a hose getting pushed down my throat." He points at his throat. "Just terrible. I wanted to fight it."

I say, "That must have been when the doctor put the ventilator back in."

"Yeah, that's what it must have been."

My son and I nod at one another.

I ask softly, "Do you remember Simon and me telling you about your dad?"

"No," Teddy says, "I don't."

I think about the many times Teddy asked, "Dad didn't make it?" And Simon and I told him, "No, Teddy, Dad didn't make it." *It's so ironic how much we worried about finding the right words to tell him, to tell Teddy. And he doesn't remember.*

"Mrs. Green, I need to speak with you."

I looked up at the young doctor who entered the small ICU room. I read the name tag on his white coat, *Dr. Donald Pierson, York Hospital.*

"What's wrong?" I asked.

"Nothing. I just need to talk with you. Please come out to the nurses' station."

I studied Teddy as I squeezed around the hospital bed. I had the impulse to kiss his cheek and hug his big shoulders, but, of course, I couldn't. IV lines curled across the rumpled green sheets to his arms; the monitor beeped with his heartbeats; the ventilator made a sing-song rhythm. I thought, *Don't stop breathing, Teddy. Whatever else is wrong, we'll face it, but don't stop breathing.*

I followed Dr. Pierson to a hallway where Simon stood sipping a cup of tea. He had never been a coffee drinker, just tea. He was only twenty-four. *He looks brave,* I thought, *and frightened. Just like me. So much like me.*

"I need to talk with you both," Dr. Pierson said. "Good news. We think it's time to try to remove the breathing tube."

"Oh," I said.

Simon tossed his cardboard cup of lukewarm tea into the nearest wastebasket. "You think it'll work this time?"

"Yes, we think Teddy's ready."

"But what if it doesn't work?" I asked.

Dr. Pierson took a long breath and said, "Teddy's twenty.

He's basically healthy. Even though he sustained a lightning strike, we're very hopeful about his prognosis. It would be irresponsible not to get him off the ventilator as soon as possible."

"So it's the right thing to do?" I asked.

"Mom," Simon said putting an arm around me and patting my shoulder. "Mom, it's good news."

"All right," I said.

"We'll go ahead then," Dr. Pierson said.

THREE DAYS BEFORE, an emergency room doctor had said to me, "I'm sorry about your husband, Mrs. Green."

"Thank you," I said. And then I expressed my worries. Was York Hospital, a small coastal outpost, the best place for Teddy? Had the staff cared for patients with lightning injuries?

"No," the ER doctor said, "none of us on the staff have ever treated lightning victims before. Most doctors haven't. But we have protocols to follow for electrical injuries." She smiled at Simon and me. "We'll take good care of Teddy."

I mouthed, "To Boston?"

"No," she said, "I don't think he should be transferred." I asked again with a frown. "No," she had said, "an unnecessary risk."

IN THE HALLWAY outside of the ICU, Dr. Pierson lowered his voice and made eye contact with Simon and me. "There is something else," he said. "Something important we need to talk about."

"What?" Simon and I asked in unison.

"Well," Dr. Pierson said, "until now, every time Teddy woke up he couldn't talk, couldn't ask questions because of the ventilator. His periods of consciousness have been brief."

Simon interrupted, "You knocked him out each time he started to ask questions. Didn't you?"

"Yes, Simon, we've done our best to delay . . ."

I cut in, "But now he can ask questions. And now he's going to ask about his dad."

"Exactly," Dr. Pierson agreed. "Now, he's sure to ask about his father. We need a plan."

"I'm his mother. I should tell him."

"I can help, Mom," Simon said.

"Fine," Dr. Pierson said. "And, of course, I can answer any medical questions."

"Oh, God," I said. *Oh God,* I thought, *help us to find the right words.*

I LOOK ACROSS the living room at Teddy. "So you don't remember anything after lunch on the little island."

"No, and nothing much in the hospital. It's like I lost a whole week of my life."

"Maybe it was psychological," I say. "Maybe your mind just closed down."

"Mom, you're such a total shrink!" Teddy says laughing. "Seriously, maybe it was just electrical."

"Maybe. I don't suppose we're ever going to know."

Teddy agrees, "We'll probably never know." We are silent for several moments.

I say, "You look really great, kid."

"I feel good, Mom. I'll try going back to school again. Maybe next year." His first effort at returning to college was frustrated by his lingering problems with concentration and memory. "But," he says, "I like my job."

"Yes, I can tell." He seems genuinely enthusiastic about working as a paramedic at a local fire station. How fortunate that Teddy had training as an emergency technician and had worked on an ambulance team before the accident and that afterward he was able to find a paramedic program to attend.

I study my son's young body. "You're really better." He nods. I remember the first days after the ventilator came out when he couldn't stand, when he couldn't walk, when he vomited up every meal. I remember the round, black burn on the back of his head and the ones above his ankles, the only visible signs of the random path of the lightning zigging and zagging through his young body ravaging nerve paths. I don't want to remind my son of any of that.

"So how's your balance. Do you still fall over every time you open the refrigerator door and lean over?"

"No," he laughs heading toward his kitchen. "D'you want a beer?"

"Sure, how about a Smuttynose? I brought some from home. It used to be your favorite."

"It still is." Teddy brings me a bottle. I look at the familiar label of a harbor seal raising its spotted head out of dark ocean depths; only its eyes and nose are above the surface. I think of its heavy, gray body hidden underwater.

That's where we are, I think. We three—Teddy, Simon, and I. The remaining family. We have our heads just barely above water, just our eyes and noses. We've just begun to grieve, and there's a lot more we can't even see.

n i n e

RIDING SHOTGUN

'm visiting Teddy on the Maryland Shore. Last night, we went to St. Michael's for hard-shell crabs and beer for dinner; it was my first experience smashing crabs with a mallet on a newspaper-covered tabletop, but I began to get the hang of it. Afterward, we were drinking tea at Teddy's when the phone rang. He strode out to the kitchen; from the living room, I overheard him saying, "Well, I can if you really need me. Sure, sure, see you in the morning."

"Someone from work?" I asked as he returned.

"Yeah, Mom. The paramedic who was scheduled to do a shift tomorrow can't make it, a death in the family." Teddy drank from his mug. "So, I said I'd go in."

"Oh, how long will you be gone?"

"I thought you could come along," Teddy said. "You're visiting. You might as well come."

"Can I?" I asked. "Is that all right?"

"Sure, Mom. You can ride shotgun," Teddy said grinning. Then, he became serious. "If there's trouble, you'll need to stay out of the way. But you can watch." I understood. I agreed.

"We better get to bed," Teddy said. "My shift starts early. You won't like that."

"Oh, I don't mind," I said.

CRO

THE NEXT DAY at the Georgetown Fire Station across the border in southern Delaware, nothing has happened. We've eaten our lunch. Teddy and Bob, the EMT on duty, are disappointed. They want me to get to share in something exciting. "Some days are like this," Bob says. "A lot of waiting. But usually even on the slowest days, we get at least one call." The three of us are relaxing, watching a sitcom on the firehouse's big TV, and drinking Coke when the alarm sounds.

"This is it, Mom," Teddy says. "You comin'?" He flips forward out of a brown faux-leather lounger with practiced skill.

"Yes," I call over to him. He is already in a bright yellow jacket and hefting a heavy bag of equipment over his shoulder. As I grab my windbreaker and my purse, I can see him breaking into a run. "Come on, Mom," he shouts back at me much like he used to when we rode horses together. Running into a behemoth of a garage, I see him throw the bag into the rear compartment of a red rescue truck and head for the driver's door.

"Here, Mrs. Green," Bob calls to me. He is holding the passenger door open for me; he gestures to the jump seat and helps me up into the cramped space.

"All set?" Teddy asks and glances back to check on me. The oversized garage door rises, and my son drives the rescue van out of the station. "Where we goin'?" he asks Bob, who is listening to garbled noise coming out of the radio. Bob responds to the disembodied voice in language that reminds me of the television shows about firemen and police our family watched when Teddy and Simon were boys.

Then, a siren sounds. Reflexively, I look behind me for an emergency vehicle. I even begin to say, "Pull over. Pull over."

"That's us, Mom," Teddy says. "We're the ones making the

noise." He laughs, a happy laugh from a proud son showing his mother his new work role. As we near a busy intersection, he says, "Look," and gestures to a button overhead. He sounds the siren, possibly a few extra times, for me to see and hear. What a joy to be riding shotgun!

Bob interprets the call we're on for me: we're taking a back road to the next town over. The police received a report of gunshots being fired at a trailer park that Bob and Teddy have been to before; we're most likely responding to a domestic violence situation. The local police are already on the scene.

Teddy drives the rescue truck with confidence, even with flair. As we cruise through intersections, as we speed past smelly chicken farms on rural back roads, I feel a palpable sense of gratitude that we two, mother and son, have been allowed to share this success together; the son who might have died, who was badly hurt, who was unable to manage in college classes, is the son who completed paramedic training and is now working in a role he embraces. He is able to support himself, to help humanity, and to enjoy the company of men like Bob, whom I like for his courtesy and hearty camaraderie. And if Teddy is not able to return to college, this is more than any of us could have imagined after Geoff died and Teddy was at York Hospital in Maine struggling to stand, to walk, to keep food down.

When we arrive at the trailer park, a policeman approaches our vehicle to advise us that the domestic incident is still underway. We are ordered not to proceed beyond a point where a fire engine from a neighboring fire station is parked. "I'll go talk to them," Teddy says and swings down to the dirt road.

As Bob and I sit in the high cab of the rescue vehicle, we can see the cautious advance of hunched policemen fanning out around an isolated trailer. The front door opens. "Look,"

Bob says pointing. Something is hurled out onto a narrow cement walkway. We hear a crash. Then, we hear one shot. I startle. "We're safe," Bob says. "We're far enough away that we're safe." Teddy comes loping back across the intersection. Then, the three of us sit and wait. "This is what it's like," Bob says, "a lot of the time. We respond, but we can't go in because it's dangerous."

"You want some?" Teddy hands me a stick of spearmint gum. I take it. It tastes good. I can't remember when I last chewed gum.

We three watch as police with drawn weapons circle then enter the trailer. Teddy points at the doorway. We see the police escort a non-descript, middle-aged man out the front door in handcuffs. A woman follows, obviously ambulatory.

"That's it," Teddy says and turns on the engine. "The guy gave himself up. We're outta' here."

"Will the police have a social worker talk with the wife?" I ask.

"Yeah, probably," Teddy says. "But she'll go back to the wack-a-doodle. You know, the crazy bastard." Teddy already sounds like a seasoned veteran. "Sorry, Mom," he says. "This work can be disillusioning."

"Yeah," I say. "My work, too."

t e n

THE OAK BOX

n the summer of 1997, three years after Geoff's death, I place a phone call.

"Lambert's Funeral Home," the receptionist answers.

"May I please speak with Ed Dickinson," I ask.

"Who shall I say is calling?"

"It's Nancy Green, Dr. Geoffrey Green's widow," I say.

I am put on hold to listen to somber music. *Brahms,* I think. Then I hear a clunk and soft whispering. I overhear a man saying, "Oh, yes." Then he picks up the phone and says, "Hello, Ed Dickinson here. How may I help you?"

"Do you remember me? Nancy Green, Geoff Green's widow." I give him a couple of seconds to recall the details from three years ago.

"Of course, I remember you, Mrs. Green." He remembers me. And Geoff. He must remember processing the paperwork to have Geoff's body shipped home across state lines in a wood particle coffin from York, Maine, to Manchester, New Hampshire; he must remember the cremation of a body that had already been sizzled by lightning.

I launch right into what I need. "Ed, could you do me a favor? My sons and Geoff's godson want to scatter his ashes off Mount Katahdin in Maine." I pause to let that sink in. I know we are late in getting around to this, but we were all stunned by Geoff's death. "I know this is a strange request." I hold my breath, but then plunge ahead, "But I need him repackaged. Do you do things like that?"

"Oh," Ed says. He pauses. "Well, sure," he says. "Sure, we can take care of that for you."

THREE YEARS EARLIER, Ed Dickinson had led me down the funeral home's wide hallway with its dark wood paneling and expensive, thick carpeting. Acanthus leaves. The pattern of the rug looked like acanthus leaves. Wasn't an acanthus leaf a traditional Greek and Roman symbol of immortality? I had been having similar random thoughts; my brain seemed to be churning out trivia to give me momentary relief from images of crackling lightning.

Ed Dickinson opened a door, and we left the refined elegance of the main floor and descended down a scuffed and steep stairway to the basement. We entered a narrow hall passing closed doors on either side. Then he paused and unlocked a door. Following his lead, I entered a large room full of open and closed caskets under the unexpected glare of blazing florescent lights.

Ed efficiently navigated his way through expensive gray and green steel caskets with me following a few steps behind. I was temporarily distracted by the white pleated satin of an open casket. Then I caught up with Ed; we entered an alcove with a discreet sign, Burial Urns.

From all the possible urns, I chose a simple oak box that I thought Geoff would have liked. Not polished brass with finials. Not walnut, pecan, or an exotic wood. But oak, which seemed fitting for a New Englander. Oak.

Although Ed Dickinson had led me away from the large

room full of caskets and into the alcove, he had not moved me far enough away. While I was choosing an urn, I was still pre-occupied with the thought that a whole formerly live human being who could have filled a coffin was now gray ash. Geoff's remains would soon be compressed inside a small wooden box no larger than the glittery jewelry box I had treasured as a girl.

SIMON AND TEDDY have both called to discuss plans. It's only a month away. In mid-August, a group of us will go to Baxter Park in central Maine and camp at Kidney Pond. My sons have happy memories of hiking and climbing with their dad. More of a bookworm than an athlete, I enjoyed hiking modest trails and have vivid memories of lady slipper, trillium, and moose sightings.

Simon has asked a friend who is studying to be a chaplain to join us, and he has volunteered to lead a service beside the lake. Then, Simon, Teddy, and Patrick, Geoff's godson, will strap on their bulging backpacks. They will carry Geoff's ashes up to Mount Katahdin, and scatter them into the wind.

MIDWAY THROUGH A phone call, Simon asks, "Mom, you've got the ashes. Don't you?"

"Yeah." I say. "They're in an oak box. You know. An urn."

"Well, they'll have to come out of the box," he says. "You'll have to take care of that. Check on how heavy they are. Maybe get them repackaged."

"Okay," I say. "Okay, I can do that." I don't say that I dread prying the box open and discovering whatever is inside.

∽ ༄ ∾

INSIDE THE BEDROOM of my high-rise condo in Manchester, I lift the oak box from my bedside table; it *is* heavy. But after all, it's a "genuine oak box with beautiful golden wood grain." But I know that it's the ashes that are heavy.

I set the box on my coverlet and turn it over. There is a screw at each corner of the bottom. I hesitate. Inhale. Exhale. But I find some courage and choose the Phillips screwdriver from my black plastic toolbox. The screw heads are stubborn. Geoff seems to be resisting my efforts to extract his ashes from the box. But I succeed; I lay the four screws on the pastel squares of my bed's quilt and flip the box upright.

Although it is a snug fit, the top of the box comes up from the bottom like the top of a fancy gift box. The bottom drops smoothly away. But instead of an anniversary present, instead of a birthday surprise, I see a bag of thick clear plastic full of gray cement-like granules—Geoff's *cremains*.

I muse over that word, *cremains*. Some mid-level marketing executive who wanted a new and neutral word for ashes or remains must have dreamed up *cremains*.

When I poke the thick plastic, it wrinkles around my forefinger. I wonder how much Geoff weighs now, and how my sons are going to carry him up Mount Katahdin. How much of him will be scattered off the Knife's Edge and what will remain for me?

ON THE PHONE with Ed at Lambert's Funeral Home, I say, "I know it's an unusual request."

"Not really," Ed says. "You would be amazed at what we're asked to do around here." I think I hear a little suppressed laughter. "Mrs. Green," he asks snapping back into his formal role, "What would you like us to do with your husband's ashes?"

"I think I'd like Geoff in four packages. Any chance you

could you do that?" I strain to explain the problem, "I think my sons want to share the burden of carrying their dad up the mountain in their backpacks."

"I understand," he says. "So four packages?"

"That would be perfect," I say.

"Give me a few hours," he says. "Drop him off, and I'll get him back to you."

I PHONE TEDDY in Maryland. "Hi, kid," I say. "I've arranged for your dad's ashes to be put in four packages."

"How much will they weigh?" he asks.

"I don't know, but lots less than just one."

THEN, I PHONE Simon in Vermont. "Simon, there will be four packages," I say. "But I think I'd like to keep one. I'm so used to having him on the bedside table."

"Mom, that's weird."

"I know, but I'm used to it."

"It's been almost three years, Mom."

"Well, you fellows can scatter the other ashes. You can carry one, Teddy, one, and Patrick can carry the other." Patrick has asked his longtime girlfriend to climb with him. "Patrick can empty his package and then ask Jillian to marry him."

"This is going to be pretty strange, Mom," Simon says.

"Life isn't simple," I say. "With one hand we scatter ashes and with the other we search for love."

"Oh, Mother," Simon is sighing. He does this a lot.

"Well, you know what I mean. Life is absurd. Your father would understand better than anyone."

"That's probably true," Simon agrees.

Three years previously, Simon and I had picked up Geoff's

ashes at the funeral home to hand-carry them to the memorial service. Simon was the one to insist that we wrap a seat belt around his "father." Simon and I drove to the church with his "dad" sitting in the back seat safely, snuggly restrained. I thought Simon was aware of the absurd.

AFTER I SPEAK with Ed, I drop off Geoff's ashes at the funeral home. Later, I receive a phone call from the concierge of my high-rise condo. "Mrs. Green," the kindly sounding gentleman says, "We have a package down here at the concierge's desk for you."

"From Lambert's?" I ask.

"Yes, from Lambert's Funeral Home. It's a cardboard box, and the gentleman who dropped it off said to tell you, 'Your hubby is ready.'" I smile at funeral home black humor.

"Thank you," I say. I take a quick elevator ride down to the lobby of my condo and retrieve a small cardboard box; inside I discover Ed's handiwork: Geoff has been repackaged in four sandwich-sized ziplock bags.

We are all set.

e l e v e n

ESCAPING GRIEF'S
KITCHEN

first had the dramatic dream, *Escaping Grief's Kitchen,* in the
fall of 1994, several months after the lightning accident.
When I awakened, I felt sad, frightened, but also curious; I
jotted down notes. Years later, I experimented with both prose
and poetry versions. The dream begins in a kitchen; I travel to
three rooms—*The Rosebud Room, The Cemetery of Claw-footed
Tubs,* and the final room where I confront *The Black Man in the
Rocking Chair.*

I AM FLOATING above a familiar kitchen; in front of me,
black and white tiles are spread out across the kitchen floor
like a diagonal game board; red sauce is smeared on the floor,
and muddy footprints crisscross the room. Below me, my son,
Simon, lifts a steaming pot while his wife, Emily, holds out a
colander. They strain the spaghetti over a cavernous sink. I
turn my face away, but when I hear the heavy pot's bottom
bump on the greasy counter, I startle. Simon swears, and I
imagine some of the stringy pasta spilling down the pipes.

Behind me in the living room, my father stands protective-
ly near my tiny mother. My husband's family forms a closed

circle; his sisters and our sister-in-law are dressed in the brittle black of New York City, his brother and our brothers-in-law are in Harris tweed jackets. My mother-in-law, even without words, communicates her usual irreverence on the occasion of the death of her younger son, my Geoff.

In the dining room, Joanna and other colleagues struggle to respect our family's grief with professional distance. They place trays of bread and carafes of red wine on a trestle table.

I float away from the kitchen island, swim away from the odors of garlic and onions, do my version of the butterfly stroke past the guest bath with its mingled scents of verbena and sandalwood. Sandalwood soap, oxford cloth shirts, baggy corduroys, and merino wool vests will all need to be packed away.

Teddy, my Teddy, dozes in a black wheelchair unaware of my passage. The prognosis is good; he will be well. Lightning has stilled his father but spared him.

I leave the apologetic and frightened expressions of my family and colleagues behind. I fly toward the unknown on sleep's wings.

ESCAPING GRIEF'S KITCHEN

Red sauce smears on black and white tiles,
muddy footprints on a chessboard floor.
My Simon asks, "Ready?"
Auburn-haired Emily nods.

A heavy pot bumps, thumps
on the greasy countertop;
he lifts the burdened pot;
she bears witness to the
colander's perforations.

Steam plunges the kitchen into fog.
Hunched deep in the sink,
Simon swears, "Oh, shit. Damn it."

His burned fingers grasp for pale gold
elbows and knees of *al dente* pasta
slipping and sliding, escaping,
disappearing into underworld pipes.
Red sauce smears on black and white tiles,
muddy footprints on the chessboard floor.

My toes lift my body up,
up inside moist air; my arms
spread into butterfly wings;
my legs morph to a mermaid's tail.
I rise, I fly, I swim
escaping grief's kitchen.

THE ROSEBUD ROOM

Down a hallway, behind the first door on the left, my floating
body discovers the dormered bedroom of a young girl. The
walls and ceiling are papered with bouquets of rosebuds, and
the small windows are blanketed with crocheted curtains.
Across from me, a narrow bed is draped with a coverlet embroidered in a grandmother's cross-stitch.

Barely inside the doorway, my body lands on the bed; my
face with eyes closed burrows like a young animal's in a primal
search for familial scent. My hands pull a shroud of worn
sheeting over me. I want to bury my head, my skull, through
the navy and white stripes of the ticking-covered mattress; I
want to dive between the soft clumps of cotton batting and to

pack it into my nose and ears and over my eyes; I want to insulate all my sensory orifices to protect myself from pain. I even want to escape from the sentimental instinct of survival. Desperate, I desire to grind my way between the grid of wire bedsprings and finally to flatten myself under the floor boards. I want to. Yes, I do.

Instead, my dream-filled eyes follow my sleepy nose to a gaping seam in the wallpaper; ordered bouquets bound tightly in blue satin bows are peeling away exposing layers of decaying paper. I feel the beginnings of nausea. Then an overpowering stench hits me—moldy layers of wallpaper upon wallpaper, crumbling plaster, rotten laths.

I realize the walls of the rosebud room have been threatened by fire, scorched, and subsequently drenched by firemen's hoses and abandoned never to truly dry. Even the thin sheets and gauzy coverlet are peppered with mildew. The bed linens have been denied the luxury of a real laundering and an afternoon on sunny clotheslines. The room has been burned and deluged; it is forever contaminated, dangerous.

I draw my nose and lungs away from the suffocation of the bedroom. But my tight chest lags behind my slowed limbs. It takes frightened, dog-like paddles to move me through the gray water of grief.

But after an eternity, my body parts—arms and legs, then lungs, gather in the hall. Shaken, I suck the water for air and the air for oxygen.

My head throbs at the loss of what seemed a possible refuge. But I close the door. Outside, I swim on.

THE ROSEBUD ROOM

Inside the Rosebud Room,
I fling myself flying
onto the single bed.

My sleepy child-self
wants to be tucked in snug.
I make a tent with sheets
and cross-stitched coverlet;
I pretend I am a child,
A forever child, sheltered
inside be-sprigged walls.

Acutely in pain, desperate,
I dive deep, deep into ticking
stripes, between the popping buttons
of the mattress. I burrow, I
bury my senses inhaling cotton
batting to still the painful news
of morning, of mourning, of death.

—2—

But even with senses muffled, I have
a healthy fear of hidden bedsprings,
of dangerous wire. I halt my deadly spiral,
retreat before a descent under floorboards
seals me in a shallow grave.

Facing the nosegays on the wall,
Smelling the rot, seeing the ragged gaps,
I'm too alive and hopeful to succumb,
to have my bones hidden behind
mildew-spotted paper, to be walled up
inside a secret grave behind broken
laths and moldy horsehair plaster.

—3—

Oh, let the firemen drag their hoses away,
go home to their wives,
go home to their sweethearts.
Oh, where's a sunny clothesline?
Let me hang my sorry, soggy self
up with wooden pegs to dry
the salt water, the tears out of me.

God, spare me the sizzle of lightning,
the pelting of rain and hail,
but save me a dewy bed of grass.
You who oppose the grieving dying young
find me a spot of sunshine.

Lay me next to a purring cat.
She will teach me contentment.
I will follow her lessons:
she will say breathe, and I shall;
she will say eat, drink, and I will.
She and I will nap until
she declares me well.

THE CEMETERY OF CLAW-FOOTED TUBS

Outside in the hallway, I bob like a hapless cork. But then with
a burst of unexpected energy, I swim rather than fly up the
back stairwell. Like some mythic female counterpart of Neptune, I make it to the third floor. Undulating past the doorways
of many anonymous cells, I am a shadowy form—hair, breasts
and fins. Far down a dim, narrow hallway, light filters through

high transoms; pale rays fall making my skin transparent; my veins appear violet. Swimming amid tangled lily pads, I press one of the doors open with the palms of my webbed hands. The large room is an artist's studio with skylights, but with no sun or blue sky; instead the slate gray of a forever February sky floats overhead. The floor is crowded with claw-footed bathtubs, tubs arranged in rows like an odd cemetery of porcelain rather than marble gravestones.

A MEMORY I promised to forget catches up with me. I choke. The rain and hail of my husband's storm are lodged in my windpipe; I am kissing a corpse. I know whose lips I kiss. Once more, I hold the pen; once more, I see the nurse's clipboard, the papers that will allow an orderly to wheel his body to the morgue. I witness again my own initials in a box and observe my disembodied hand scrawl my signature. And I imagine my pen performing an autopsy.

THE CLAW-FOOTED tubs that crowd the room are empty, useless, bereft. From my aerial glide, I search for water and bathers, but instead I see irregular mineral pools; blue and green poison burn into the porcelain leaving crusty grains of misery and danger.

As I hover above the cemetery of claw-footed tubs, I raise my eyes and study the vertical piping as it climbs toward the ceiling; it fails only inches short of the couplings near the ceiling. *Pipes and fittings*, I think. *Never, never to meet.*

I wonder at the horizontal snakes of piping that make shadows upon the walls; they are like the crests of shallow waves rising toward remembered thighs and then dipping to absent knees. I study the pipes suspended in mid-air; for moments, I am one with the pipes, caught in a trance like a weary dancer.

From my floating position, I view the porcelain tubs eternally waiting for bathers and imagine them as multiple marble graves with the inscription, GEOFFREY CHAUCER GREEN. I envision them across the innumerable anniversaries ahead.

At the doorway, my sea-blue eyes follow the length of each forlorn pipe to its natural conclusion. I laugh at the irony. I weep salty tears at the loss. I know I need to go.

I cannot remain in the Cemetery of the Claw-footed Tubs. I take one last look at the bones. Swim to the door. And slam it shut with a kick of my webbed feet.

THE CEMETERY OF THE CLAW-FOOTED TUBS

Overhead transoms transform me;
unworldly light colors my veins violet.
My webbed hands swim inside an eerie loft,
its slippery floor covered with row
upon row of claw-footed tubs.
Surely, claw-footed tombs.

No water, no bathers in these tubs,
but rusty rings around and around,
and inside, only remnant pools
in this porcelain. Grainy mineral crusts,
an unholy sulphuric green. Even in
my fog, I know a claw-footed cemet'ry.

Mid-stroke, I study the orphan
pipes rising and bending but
always ending abruptly. No fittings.
No fitting ending for these pipes.
No conduit for healing water.
Lead in color. And leaden.

—2—

As I exit, I cry out, "Oh, my Neptune,
oh, my bather and dancer in life's waves,
what has stilled your splashing limbs?
What has become of your artful pose?
Or are you too sizzled, too soddened
to raise your mighty trident?"

THE BLACK MAN IN THE ROCKING CHAIR

Leaving the Cemetery of the Claw-Footed Tubs, I am spent. But I find my way to the third-floor landing and fall, a formless heap against an upholstered seat. When I sit up, I am facing a great stained-glass window of weeping willows.

Later, after I collect my courage and strength, I roll down the stairway to the second floor. I tumble from a world of weary wet to one of welcome dry, landing on a splendid carpet runner of gold, green, and red silk.

At an open doorway, I stumble to my feet. In what appears to be a warehouse of antiques, sofas, tables, and chairs are arranged in pseudo-rooms. I stride into the space with a determination that surprises me. I am searching for whatever I am supposed to discover next. My bare feet follow a worn path, soft as fine sand.

I pass Victorian sofas and chairs with plush mounds of fabric secured by covered buttons. I squeeze through rows of high-backed dining room chairs. I pursue my goal, the farthest corner, a dimly lit alcove. In a Kennedy rocker, a black man sits. So still? Is he sleeping? His spine is pressed against oak slats, his buttocks rest on woven rush. His open palms are outstretched into the air on either side like a black cormorant drying his feathers. He appears like some lesser saint who deserves a rocking chair rather than a cross.

As I approach, I smell the stench of burning flesh. I know then that I am not in the presence of a black man but a blackened man burned by a strike of lightning. My mind asks its questions: Why did he die? How was Teddy spared? But I think I know. I make a modest Buddhist bow to the black man and whisper, "Namaste." I am thanking him for his sacrifice.

I HOPE THAT during the half-day, the twelve hours that Geoff's heart was revived and continued to beat after the accident, he knew that I wished him Godspeed. It was all I knew to hope for—that wish and the ironic opposite that he had known no consciousness at all. Is life always the hypothesis and the antithesis?

IN THE MOMENT that I stand before Geoff, I hope he knows that I have not only come to pay my respects, but that I also have to leave. I have to live.

I stand sober, collected, and resolved.

My head bowed, I whisper, "Geoffrey Chaucer Green. I forgive you. Forgive me." And with that simple prayer behind me, I weave between the peculiar furniture and walk out of the alternative world.

THE BLACK MAN IN THE ROCKING CHAIR

I escaped grief's kitchen, flew into the
moldy mildew of the rosebud room,
eschewed diving under deadly floorboards
to wither a child forever. Fleeing, I

swam upstairs to a silvery world
only to abandon the doomed pursuit
of love in the arms of a dead man.

Now, I face the blackened body
of Geoff, who sits not any known martyr
but some lesser saint, arms spread out
like weary wings, resting in a rocker,
no JFK, but my sons' hero, my gone
husband waiting for his last audience.
I bow, whisper, "Namaste." Peace.

No journey's destiny so unexpected
as this one where what is feared is faced,
and fears faced, the night's odyssey—
part dream, part nightmare, ends.

Dream over, my eyes open. My fists relax, and I examine
the nail prints dug into my palms with curiosity. My thin ring-
less hands brush away the sleep, the teary deposit in the corners
of my eyes. Morning filters through my organdy curtains illu-
minating the photos of my sons on my dresser, and across the
room, the oak box of Geoff's ashes rests on the rush seat of a
Kennedy rocking chair.

Bella, my companion, my cat, raises her head. She stretches
her body to its full length. Sinuous, she is my beauty.

My arduous overnight travel has served its purpose. I vow
to bury Geoff's urn and move his rocking chair to the guest
room. I raise my head off the cross-stitched pillowcase that my
Grandmother Lucy embroidered. I kick aside the sheets I've
been tangled in all night. My body rises. . . .

t w e l v e

ONE QUARTER

OF THE ASHES

I felt compelled to move after the lightning accident; each new location only fit me for a while. For six months, I rented a condo convenient to Concord Hospital. Then I bought a high rise condo in Manchester; small, less than 1000 square feet; it provided a concierge to greet me and covered parking; its security and little luxuries served me well. I liked living at tree-top level just a block from the Victorian house where Geoff and I had worked together in a group private practice with fellow psychologists and social workers. That magical span of ten years at Green House Group had been happy for me, and I'm sure my choice of home was influenced by an unconscious desire to be near Geoff.

Three years after his death, I traded the tiny high-rise in Manchester for a condo in Chester, New Hampshire. Now I had a proper guest room for my sons; Simon was especially glad to graduate from a Murphy bed. My moves were along the arc of a compass—first West of Deerfield, then Southwest, then South, but never more than thirty miles from our family home. The woman who lived in each home was me, but a slightly different version of me as I made uneven progress through the passageways of grief.

Chester, a rural village, offered colonial charm and relative anonymity. I adopted a basset hound named Molly, and she and I took walks along a stream with a beaver dam. "Look," I would say to her, and she would stop snuffling along the path and point her nose at the odd brown creatures swimming with sticks in their mouths. Chester was much like Deerfield without being Deerfield.

An elderly Jewish psychiatrist, genial and kind, invited me to join the private practice he supervised nearby; Molly accompanied me to my work setting an example of calm as she slept next to my desk. I even joined a book club of boisterous women who met around one another's kitchen tables. My life was wending toward normal.

During the time I lived in Chester, I met Jackson at a birthday party for a mutual friend; we started talking books. He was a village librarian, significantly younger than I was, with the baggage of a painful divorce. But he was bright and single and just what I needed.

On a Saturday afternoon in November, the sun is setting early in southern New Hampshire. I pull up the silky straps of my nightgown and lean back against the oak headboard of my four poster. Jackson is lying next to me covered with a sheet to his waist but with his chest and its distinctive curly red hair exposed.

He asks, "Sweetheart, don't you think it's about time you moved Geoff out of your bedroom?"

"Move him?" I stare across the master bedroom at a Kennedy rocking chair; for many years, Dr. Geoff Green, my deceased husband and psychologist, sat in the chair listening to patients, nodding his head in therapeutic empathy. Now an oak box containing his ashes "sits" in the chair. Since his death, the box has been an integral part of my bedroom décor.

"I suppose I could move him," I say. "I didn't even know you noticed."

Jackson sighs. Of course, he noticed. Every time we made love, he must have felt Geoff was sitting in the bedroom.

"It's not really Geoff you know," I explain. "Well, not all of him. It's only one quarter of his ashes."

"What?" Jackson frowns.

"Don't you remember? I explained it to you."

"Tell me again."

"Most of Geoff is on Mt. Katahdin," I say. "Simon and Teddy scattered him off the Knife's Edge."

"The Knife's Edge?"

"Mm-hmm," I say. "But just three quarters of him. I kept one quarter." I kick off the sheets, pull on a flannel robe and walk across the room to the south-facing window. Tying the belt of my robe, I peer out. It's turning dark although it's only four o'clock. I pick up the oak box and sit down on the rush seat of the rocker. Holding the ashes on my lap, I strain to act with the maturity of a widow who has already passed through many of the supposed stages of grief.

"I guess I could move him to the guest room," I say.

I hear Jackson murmur something and look at him. He is an old-fashioned looking man. I like the effect of his tonsure surrounded by red hair and his wispy mustache. And I enjoy his enthusiasms, especially his fascination with the Battle of Gettysburg. I think he looks like a real Civil War soldier, a Union officer, in his reenactment uniform.

WHEN I WAS eight years old, my father, a high school history teacher, insisted on taking me to Gettysburg. We walked the battlefield together; it was important to my dad that I understand the great loss of life. "The creeks ran red with blood," he told me somberly. I saved the words and images to remember later. Sometimes, I think that my father has sent me Jackson to comfort me and to talk to me about how men and women summon courage under fire.

"WHAT?" JACKSON ASKS.

"I said I'm going to move Geoff."

"That would be great," he says.

I look up prepared to catch him being a smart ass, but he is perfectly serious.

"I'll move him. Right now," I say.

I carry the box to the large bathroom that serves both bedrooms. I check the woman in the mirror—thin and pale but better off than during the first years after Geoff's death. I smooth my cap of red hair. No reason to put lipstick on; Jackson will just kiss it off.

As I pass through the bathroom, I think, *Geoff, I'm moving you to the guest room. It's nice. You'll like it. Actually more masculine. I decorated it for the boys when they come home.*

I exit the bathroom and carry the box against my chest into the guest room. At the foot of the queen-sized bed with its iron frame, I pause and place the box on the navy and white striped quilt, the one I created using yards of family ticking. Geoff's family, an old German Jewish family in New York City, manufactured textiles, specifically mattress ticking.

In 1968, when we were courting, Geoff told me about his family's business. I remember saying, "Well, making ticking for mattresses should be a dependable business as long as people go on sleeping." I wasn't a funny person, but I tried occasionally to be humorous. Now I don't try often. Life rarely seems funny. Odd. Weird. Sad. Absurd. But not funny.

I tell Geoff, *You'll be comfortable here.* Then, with a big inhalation and exhalation, I walk out of the guest room, step across the hallway and slowly open the door of the master bedroom.

"I did it," I announce to Jackson. "Geoff's moved."

"Good work," Jackson says. He looks at me carefully. "Come back to bed. I missed you. You were gone for a long time."

"No, I wasn't," I protest.

"I know you, and I think you were gone a long time and that you went far away."

"You do know me," I say.

I climb into bed, pull up the duvet, and turn out my bedside lamp. I wipe tears away with the corner of the top sheet before I turn to face Jackson.

"Let me hold you," he says. "You've been working hard. I think you need some hugs."

"I suppose you wonder why I haven't buried Geoff's ashes," I ask.

"I do wonder," Jackson says. "There's an old and beautiful cemetery here in Chester. It's historic. Anyone would be glad to be buried here."

"Oh, Jackson," I laugh. "You do say things that would sound odd to anyone but me."

"It's the oldest cemetery in New Hampshire," he says. "There are graves dating back to before the Revolutionary War. I can imagine being happy buried there."

And I know he is being serious. He particularly would like to be tucked into the soil of an old cemetery because in his heart he is living in the wrong century. He is a Victorian. Maybe I am too. We both like brave heroes, beautifully written letters, and old courtly manners.

I say, "But, I do, I do think the Chester Cemetery is lovely. Just not quite right for Geoff."

"And you're not quite ready."

"Not quite." I say, "Thanks for understanding."

"How do you feel about kisses?"

"I like kisses, especially yours. Your mustache tickles."

Jackson reaches out and turns off the hobnail glass lamp on his side of the bed. Across the room, a nightlight made of shells casts soft light on the striped wallpaper.

"I like a little light on at night," I confess.

"I know," Jackson whispers. "Sometimes there are storms, storms with hail and thunder and lightning; sometimes there are accidents that shock us."

He stops speaking for a second. "Sorry," he says. "What I mean is I know you like a little light on. It's okay with me. You don't have to apologize."

"I like you, Jackson."

"I hope so."

DREAM NUMBER 1,
DRIVING WITH GEOFF

F our, maybe five years after Geoff's death, I have a surprising dream:

Reclining in the passenger seat of my white Saturn, I peer
out from under my favorite baseball hat as the car passes a great
blur of flowering trees bright with pink blossoms. The sun is
warm on my cheek; the car's shoulder harness tugs across my
chest. I have the foggy awareness that something is wrong.

Later, still feeling drowsy, almost heavy, my eyes blink
open and close several times. Blocks of attractive, clapboard-
sided houses with a scattering of stone churches, handsome
with steeples, buzz by. *I must be in New England,* I think. *Probably
somewhere in Massachusetts. Maybe, Newburyport? Or Portsmouth,
New Hampshire?*

Then later, the storefronts of small businesses—restaurants, dry cleaners, and bakeries, whiz by. Signs advertise pizza
and donuts. My fuzzy mind registers that now there is less
open space, more congestion. The car should be slowing down,
stopping at lights and crosswalks. But it isn't.

I feel uneasy. Even a little nauseous. I sit up abruptly, pull
off my hat. I glance at the driver of the car. It is Geoff. Geoff,
my *late* husband. Late as in dead.

Geoff is driving in a crowded downtown area. He should be slowing. But instead, he's accelerating. I turn toward the driver's seat. I'm curious to see what Geoff looks like, but also frightened. What does a man who has been dead for five years look like? So I avoid making eye contact.

I say as evenly as I can, "This driving isn't a good idea, Geoff."

He ignores me. So much like Geoff. He speeds around a rotary.

This time I'm more firm. "Geoff, it would be better if I drove." I pause. "I'm a good driver." No response from him.

Finally, I am fierce. Fierce for me. "Geoff, you've been dead for five years. You should let me drive!"

Geoff disappears. No one is at the wheel.

"Jesus, Geoff!" I swear. He can be so impulsive. "Come back. You can pull over. We'll trade places."

Geoff returns to the car and resumes driving. But instead of pulling over, he suddenly brakes in the middle of an intersection. He just disappears! I am surrounded by honking cars, tooting trucks; drivers are yelling, swearing at me. I scramble over the awkward center console, search for the foot pedals and grab the steering wheel.

"Damn you, Geoff!" I cry out in the empty car.

But I *am* in the driver's seat. And I *am* a good driver.

ONLY IN A dream does a late husband pop up in the driver's seat and then vanish. What does it mean? Frankly, I think it is a message from my subconscious to take charge of my life. After all, Geoff *is* dead.

f o u r t e e n

TRIAGE AND COWS

I n May of 1999, nearly five years have passed since what we in the family, we three survivors, call "the accident." Simon and Emily are living in Fremont, California, near San Francisco where Simon is a graduate student at UCSF. I'm in Baltimore visiting Teddy who is nearing graduation in Emergency Services at UMBC.

"THE POOR COWS," I say. It's out of my mouth before I can call it back. I wonder if Teddy has heard me.

Someone else, a female undergrad, says, "Poor things."

Then, I don't feel so foolish about my outburst. The image of the cows is still on the screen at the front of the classroom.

The five cows lie beside a barbed wire fence that slices diagonally across the photo. Legs deep in soggy marsh, the beasts were vulnerable to a lightning strike. Now the Holsteins appear like black and white blobs of paint, two-dimensional figures having lost the vigor of being three-dimensional.

I strain to see. Is the photo blurred or are the cows bloated and their deaths so gaseous that the air is fogged?

Teddy clicks the remote and the next photo appears. A relief.

He is midway through his presentation on "The Successful Triage and Treatment of Electrical Injuries." He has already covered the protocol for the assessment of injuries. His fellow upper classmen and I have followed along as he described the possible bodily systems impacted by electrical accidents.

In laymen's terms, electricity can cause your heart to stop, your breathing to cease, your skin to be burned, and your nerves to fray. Then, there's blunt trauma force. How could I forget that? And injuries to eyes and ears. And of course, electricity can kill you.

I hope the class understands in more sophisticated terms than I do what they should examine and treat. But I can sense that all of us are being emotionally affected by Teddy's presentation.

He has shown us photos of horrific burns on the chests and backs of male power company employees. Now photos of lightning hitting trees, buildings, and airplanes alert us to a section about statistics, more statistics than we can absorb. To be brief, in the US, most lightning injuries and deaths occur in Texas and Florida. To males between fifteen and nineteen. Between May and September. In a typical year in the US, three hundred victims will be injured by lightning, but only one hundred will die. And in the rest of the world, Uganda is a country where lightning injuries and deaths are high for no discernable reason.

Teddy reminds us that while lightning hits the Earth often, people are rarely injured or killed. Getting hit by lightning *is* rare. The odds *are* one in a million.

Then he returns to the photo of the cows, the black and white puddles of paint. The surreal image.

TEDDY INVITED ME to come see this presentation. He will graduate in a month, and I will travel again to Baltimore to witness his graduation, an achievement once unimaginable.

Today, he and I arrived early. He settled me in a desk at the rear of the classroom. He opened his laptop and confirmed that he could summon up information and images on the screen. I sat quietly as his fellow students filed in. His professor introduced himself, and I was friendly but restrained. I hoped to be a model mother.

This is Teddy's day. Usually I am weary of professional PowerPoint presentations, but Teddy's use of carefully chosen photos enliven his teaching. Plus, I think I know where he is heading.

Still, I am surprised when a yellowed newspaper clipping appears on the screen. A Portsmouth, New Hampshire headline crisscrossed with crease marks proclaims, "FATHER AND SON HIT BY LIGHTNING."

The classroom is still. I can hear the hum of the air conditioning. I hold my breath. Teddy clicks the remote. I breathe.

The next image is an excerpt from a patient's chart dated July 23, 1994. It is Teddy's chart. Upon his arrival at the emergency room of York Hospital at approximately 4:05 p.m., his feet had no pulse and appeared purple. Two hours later after receiving treatment, he had a pulse in his feet, and they appeared pink.

"I was hit by lightning," Teddy tells his classmates. Some might have known, but I don't think many of them did. His professor nods at me. He knew.

Teddy zeroes in. He says, "Triage in the treatment of electrical victims is different from what you're used to. Among multiple victims, one may appear to be a lost cause—no heartbeat, no breathing." He makes eye contact with each of us. "But," he says, "in the case of a power accident or a lightning

strike, the unconscious victim without a pulse may be saved."
He stops. We all look up. He begins again. "If you don't remember anything else from this presentation, remember this: triage in the case of electrical injuries needs to be counter-intuitive. Treat the victim who appears to be a lost cause. He or she often can be saved."

Teddy knows.

When Teddy and his father were discovered on the concrete floor of a WWI bunker at Fort Foster on the Maine coast, both he and his dad appeared dead. Both appeared two-dimensional. Teddy's father did die. But Teddy rose from a two-dimensional puddle to fully inhabit his life. He rose. He is my miracle. He will always be my miracle.

Teddy clicks the remote. The screen becomes blank. His classmates shake his hand, thump him on his back. His professor walks to me. I wipe at my tears and compose myself.

f i f t e e n

STONE HOUSE

On a warm July morning in 2001, I leave Portland, Maine, drive north on Route One, and turn right at the big wooden Indian, a local landmark. I follow the back road into South Freeport, which was settled early and is dotted with Colonial-era homes. I pause and marvel at a herd of Belted Galloways, remarkable black and white striped cows. Then, I hurry through the thick woods of Wolfe Neck's peninsula following signs to the University of Southern Maine's Summer Writers' Conference. I park my car beside a barn and hurry up the steps between the pillars of Stone House.

By 9:00 a.m., I am on the second floor standing in a classroom. For a few moments, I stare out a wide window at a steep slope of tall grass obscuring the view of a nearby tidal inlet. Perhaps unconsciously, I strain to see kayaks pulled up on the nearby sandy banks.

That's probably all I am aware of at first—the tidal water in the distance. When I submitted my story and application for the conference, I was intent upon the deadline; the dates of the conference didn't compute. It is the third week of July, and I have been excited and anxious about participating in a program for serious writers led by published authors. This morning, my focus has been on following the directions and arriving on time.

Only later will I question my judgment of attending a conference on the seventh anniversary of the lightning accident. The truth is that even though time has passed, I never know when something will occur that will bring back a rush of painful memories and completely distract me from what is happening in the present.

I place a notebook and pen on the cloth-draped surface of the conference table and sit in a utilitarian chair. I face my workshop leader. That's when Michael Manfried says it. Not much else happens before he says, "Sometimes, lightning strikes. It strikes, and a writer has no choice. He or she has been chosen to write."

In the next moment, Michael is identifying himself as a writer and editor from New York City and saying, "Please introduce yourselves. Please share whatever comes into your mind." And my thoughts are spinning around inside my brain like golden fizz, and I'm wondering, *what the devil am I going to say to these strangers?*

I decide quickly that it will not be what is on my mind. I won't lie; that's not me, but I will share mundane information. "I'm Nancy," I say. "I was born in Montana. My mother taught English." I probably say some other bullshit.

I try to listen to Michael, but I am distracted. Later when I can't bear anymore, I duck out to go to the bathroom. On my return, I study the framed maps of the Maine Coast in the hallway, maps not only of Wolfe's Neck Peninsula but also of other Maine coastline fingers and islands drawn by mapmakers between 1830 and 1840.

But while I examine the various maps, my mind travels back to July 23, 1994. And I search for maps of Portsmouth Harbor, Kittery Point, and Gerrish Island. I envision the early signs of a hostile storm. Sea kayaks are being hurriedly pulled up on the beach at Fort Foster on Gerrish Island. Figures in swimsuits are running for shelter as a freak summer storm targets its random rage on the tiny island. Angry black clouds empty torrents of rain; knuckle-sized hail hits my husband and younger son.

And as I stare at the hand-colored maps, my imagination sees a streak of gold and smoky-gray lightning cross the unsuspecting sky. Geoff peers out the rectangular slit in the concrete wall of a WWI bunker; Teddy stands a step or two behind him. Attracted by the skeletal steel girders of the anti-submarine watch post, a spear of fiery electricity shoots through the previously picnic-like day and penetrates Geoff and Teddy; it leaves them prostrate on the stone cold floor.

When I return to the classroom, it is time for lunch break. Walk with me from the upstairs as I step down the stairway. Watch my right hand as it skims the polished surface of the railing. My eyes are lowered watching the turned balustrades alternate beside my bare legs. At the landing, I turn. A stained-glass window at my back, I continue to the first floor.

In the carpeted reception room, aspiring writers and their workshop leaders move in slow motion around me. Beside walls bordered with painted wainscoting and crown moldings, writers undulate in paisley patterns of conversation. Between a silver-plated coffee urn and a small pitcher of heavy cream, the string of a discarded teabag is wound around and around a teaspoon which lies upside down. I am mesmerized. I reach out to touch the stain on the table linen. It is brown and damp.

Walk with me as I slip out through a book display to the front door. Near the entry, I pause and take several slow breaths in and out, sifting for salt or seaweed. The breeze feels fresh, welcome. Aware of my slowed breathing, I admire the generous porch that extends the whole front of Stone House, a former estate, a gift to the university. A dusting of flaking paint has accumulated at the bottom of a pillar, and I kick idly at it. After a few swipes, I restrain myself.

In the next moments, I stride with feigned purpose across the carelessly mown grass of the front yard, and pass writers sitting at picnic tables and in Adirondack chairs. A sleeping yellow Labrador groans as I pass. But the short path ends abruptly at a giant outcropping of granite ledge; around and among the rocks of the mound-shaped obstacle, Scottish heather grows in stubborn tufts.

Toward the open sea, high underbrush, too thick for me to navigate in my sandals, blocks my passage, but beyond that, the rhythmic waves of the North Atlantic pound the stones of the beach into sand. I retreat back to the porch; only my ears can confirm the ocean's presence; the watery grave of so many is out of sight. It's time to grab a cardboard cup of caffeine and rejoin my workshop. Return with me.

I'M SITTING IN my rigid chair smiling and nodding as though I am like anyone else, an ordinary person with bland secrets. And I'll be damned if Michael doesn't do it again. "My computer crashed this morning," he says. "I got it going, and it crashed again. Imagine lightning striking twice in the same place."

And I do. I imagine lightning striking twice, once through Geoff's chest incinerating his heart and lungs and then flashing through Teddy's head, pulsing through his body and exiting above the heels of his sneakers. And I listen for Teddy's heart to beat on its own. Geoff's won't. I've accepted that.

How oddly the four conference tables in the Map Room are arranged; they create a rectangle with a casket-sized shape of emptiness remaining in the center. Each one of us sits prayerfully with our hands resting on draped damask. The white "flags" cover every table, and we squirm in awkward chairs like children on church pews or relatives in folding chairs at a crowded funeral parlor.

I reach back and turn on a silver rotating fan to move the air, to interrupt the stillness, and to dilute the lemony smell of furniture polish. And then I notice the fireplace; the ochre tiles of the hearth are crackled and blackened and the remains of ash in the grate have been stirred up by the circulating air. Twisting in my chair, I turn the switch of the fan to low. Now my gaze travels to the mantle, and I am surprised by flowers, lavender asters and willowy Queen Anne's lace, in a pressed glass vase. Have they been there all the time?

I stare out the window at the view of the grassy hillside looking for the shadowy figure of whoever brought the flowers. Frustrated, my eyes strain to see kayaks on a faraway shore.

THEN I TURN my attention back inside the room. I am concentrating now, and believe it or not, Mike Manfried, my nonfiction workshop leader, has managed not to say lightning for two hours.

GROWING OUT
OF GRIEF

Maine's coastal sky spits gray, thin rain
along the miles of sprawling cove;
I could rise in the raw drizzle,
stumble to my modest cottage,
but the weather is my mood;
it suits, therefore calms,
the fog nothing to the storm I've known.

I lie face-down on the beach's wet sand,
no blanket, no towel;
my face hidden in my slicker's sleeve;
a mottled hound huddles at my ribs;
wet, still we sleep till she whines,
I whimper; she leads me home.

—2—

My body burrows in the sun-warmed earth,
a cheek against a mound of palest tan;
I nurse at the primeval breast,
a celebrant in some surprising rite,
belly tethered to a constant source,

a babe tied to her whole world's cord.
I fiercely love my new birth mother—
new guardian, new lover, even new god.

I walk on consecrated ground
where sky, sea, shore meet,
where incised discs of shell lay strewn,
where shorebirds twitter on twig-like legs.
I'm witness to a sudden miracle:
a flock of plover swirl, a triangle of flight;
then another wonder, they return.
I'm growing out of grief.

—3—

I wade knee deep in tepid tidal pools
reminiscent of the ocean of my birth;
ankle deep, I plod dreamily along
through Goose Rock's shallow surf;
kicking up splashes of sky-blue sea,
I'm outgrowing grief.

After ill-timed deaths—husband, father,
a fiery shock, the near-death of a son,
after my innumerable protests of "I'm all right,"
years pass, fears subside, hopes revive, I'm
like a child outgrowing socks and shoes;
the hems of my pant legs—too short, need letting down.
Thanks to my love of holy ground
I'm growing out of grief.

seventeen

DREAM NUMBER 2,
DEAD WEIGHT

Twelve years after Geoff's death, during a time when I was working at Maine Medical Center in Portland, Maine, as a psychiatric social worker and awaiting shoulder replacement surgery, I had this dream.

I AM FLYING fine, flying high above a forest, but I descend too quickly. Suddenly, the tops of evergreens come charging up at me; I barely avoid several sharp pine spikes. And then, with my pajamas flapping, I am rushed into choosing a place to come down. Unfortunately, my body makes a clumsy landing on what Arthur Conan Doyle would have called a stony hillock.

That's when a train crashes. I hear a great explosion, see giant sparks and yes, hear moans and screams. I run down a steep hillside stumbling, falling. Then I struggle to my feet, run forward and get tangled in the thorny branches of a high, thick hedge. With my hands in front of my face, I force myself to keep going.

Move, you sleepy fool, I say to myself. *Someone is counting on you.*

My hands and forearms are bleeding, but I push through the thicket. I can barely see in the thick smoke, but I can smell burned flesh. My mind is alert. This is serious business; this is about life and death.

In the gray and brown haze, I see two figures. One is standing, looking around. He sees a fuel tank nearby and is gesticulating and yelling to someone on the ground to get up. I can tell from his frantic movements that he thinks there is going to be another explosion.

As he turns away, I can see that he has no clothes on the upper part of his body; his back is bright red. In a flash, I say to myself, *He's been burned. He's in pain.* But I don't say anything. Nothing aloud. Even in my dream. I just watch too sobered by what I am witnessing to speak. Besides, I'm a New Englander; we don't say much.

The man with the burned back is able to walk and moves away from me into the smoky distance. But the other victim lies unmoving on the gravel at my feet. He is helpless. He is my job. I am supposed to get him up and out before another explosion and without anyone seeing me.

I think, *That's what I do at night in my dreams. I do what is needed. Invisibly. I'm not big or strong. That's not how I fly or save people. I do it the same way I ride horses; I fly thanks to courage and balance.*

I sling the man over my left shoulder and grip him with my arms. Once clear of the tracks, I am faced with getting up. I can't fly as I usually do so I levitate. Not much altitude at first, but off the ground. I just need to get away from the explosion and out of sight. I keep repeating to myself, *It shouldn't have happened. It shouldn't have happened.* But how does that help?

I fly in my awkward fashion for hours and hours. Late in the afternoon, I look down at the farm I am flying over; the grasshopper weathervane looks familiar. My left shoulder is in terrible pain. I'm exhausted, and the man hasn't moved. I can't tell if he is warm anymore. I was sweaty before; now with the sun going down, I feel cold. No matter who he is, it's time for me to go to ground. I guess that's when I let the idea dawn on me. I may be carrying a dead man. *Think about it,* I tell myself. *Has he moved? Does his body feel warm?* I answer myself. *No. He feels like dead weight.*

I land in the vegetable garden of the farm below me. I find a barn and inside the barn, a beautiful jersey cow. "You're a fine cow," I tell her and gently pat her velvety hindquarters." I need some sleep," I say. "Would you mind sharing your hay with me?"

I roll Geoff onto the floor next to the feed room. "I think you're Geoff," I say. "And I think you're dead. Whoever you are, I don't think lying in a barn will hurt you. And I can't carry you any farther."

Your husband, Geoff, has been dead a long time, my dream-self, my sub-conscious says, *You've been carrying dead weight around all this time in reality and in this dream. And it's no damn wonder your left shoulder's broken; it's no wonder you're in pain. Your shoulder gets tired carrying so much weight, and it's broken. It just stopped working; now you have to stop, too. Stop carrying Geoff; he's dead weight.*

And it's all true; during one night's sleep, I've psychoanalyzed myself.

e i g h t e e n

FORT FOSTER

In the past twenty years, I've been to Fort Foster on Gerrish Island many times. The fortifications including Battery Chapin, the site of the lightning accident, were built in 1902 to protect Portsmouth Harbor and the Portsmouth Naval Shipyard. Fort Foster was deactivated in 1948 and the land was given to the town of Kittery, Maine, to be used as a park. Its ninety-eight acres lie near the border of New Hampshire with Maine. The park offers the following attractions: a stone pier, several beaches, and picnic areas as well as fine views of Whaleback Light and the Wood Island Lifesaving Station. The pretty island-park seems a most unlikely location for a tragic accident.

My first visit to Fort Foster was in July of 1995, a year after Geoff died. I wanted to pay my respects on the anniversary of his death, but I was also looking for answers. My friend, Jules, drove us from Manchester, New Hampshire. Before I knew it, we were in Portsmouth crossing the Piscataqua River Bridge into Maine; we left the highway at the Kittery Exit. Jules knew the area, but it was all new to me. Soon, we were on a narrow winding road, passing pretty homes including a handsome historical house, and then we were at Captain Simeon's Galley. As we ate burgers and drank beer, I looked out at the view, a lighthouse.

"It's Whaleback Light," Jules said. "That's where we're headed." He pointed into the distance. "That's Fort Foster."

"Really?" I asked. I remember how I felt—unprepared that this beautiful sight on a blue-sky day was the location of the fatal lightning accident. The stations along the rest of the ride, the Chauncey Creek Lobster Pound, the narrow bridge to Gerrish Island, and the entrance booth to the park, were so normal. And that was confusing.

My memories of visits to Fort Foster are a bit of a blur because of my tears. Years after my first visit, I went with Jackson in the rain. He was a kind man, and I remember him holding an umbrella over me and steadying me as we climbed the big and awkward cement steps of Battery Chapin. It was impossible not to think of rain and hail pelting down on the rescuers as they rushed up the steps and ladder to the bunker. And I am still puzzled by how they could have carried my husband and son, both big men, down the maze of obstacles to the waiting ambulances from the towns of Berwick and Eliot.

The bunker itself is small and cramped, concrete with rusted beams and railings. It feels tomb-like. Rather like a mausoleum. Just as it should.

Over time, I developed rituals. I would take a bouquet of daisies to the park; daisies were Geoff's favorite flower although he was also fond of irises. I would walk down the long pier and throw one daisy at a time onto the surface of the slow-moving tide.

One year, I went with the women of my book club on a ferry ride out of Portsmouth Harbor around the Isles of Shoals. It was a breezy July day, and I took along a wreath of daisies to throw into the ocean. We had read Anita Shreve's novel, *The Weight of Water*, set in Portsmouth and on Smuttynose Island.

I knew that the ferry stopped at Star Island, passed near Smuttynose, and stopped again on Appledore for tours of the house and garden of the nineteenth-century poet Celia Thaxter.

I wasn't sure how close the boat would get to Fort Foster, but it turned out that it swept past the bunker and the beach. I threw the wreath out of the boat on the port side, and it came flying back on the wind to me. How surprising and even alarming that was. So next, I tried the starboard side. By now what had seemed a small private act had attracted many of the ferry passengers' attention. I was determined to be rid of the wreath. The second time I threw hard; the wreath fell between small waves, and within moments, the ferry passed it by. Sometimes, I think, *It's not easy to leave grief behind; it is flung back at you when you least expect it.*

Another ritual I found helpful was to read Jewish prayers from a Reform prayer book; while Geoff had been a secular Jew, the prayers helped me feel close to him. On visits to Fort Foster, I would climb inside the bunker and set the prayer book on the concrete ledge of the large slit-shaped window. Facing Whaleback Light and the picturesque but decaying US. Coast Guard Life-Saving Station, I could see the open ocean and recite:

O God, this hour revives in us memories of loved ones who are no more. . . .
We see them now with the eye of memory, their faults forgiven,
Their virtues grown larger.
So does goodness live, and weakness fade from sight.
We remember them. . . .
As we remember them, let us meditate on the meaning of love and loss,
Of life and death.

May the Source of peace send peace to all who mourn,
And comfort to all who are bereaved.
Amen.

From *Gates of Prayer, The New Union Prayer Book*, New York:
Central Conference of American Rabbis, 1975.

The last time I was at Fort Foster, it was with David, a dear friend. We said the prayers together. He was Jewish and able to recite the *Mourner's Kaddish* in Hebrew. As we left, the sun was beginning to set; the sky was ivory and many shades of gray and gold. Often in Maine, the skies are so unbelievably lovely that if an artist painted them, no one would believe they were real.

And that is how my visits to Fort Foster have been. So surreal.

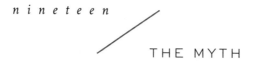

n i n e t e e n

THE MYTH

Geoff, I've never seen the medical and police records from the accident, and I've been thinking of writing for them. I think it's time. After all, it's been many years. And I think I could read them now, the vital signs of our family's accident. Tell me if you're ready. I'll write York Hospital and the Kittery Police in Maine. And we'll see what comes.

I'm full of questions I wish I could ask you. In the Emergency Room, were you dead? All the time? And how close did Teddy come to slipping over the edge? And why wasn't I the one to die? Why wasn't I the one to be scraped off the pavement like Chubb Chubb, our Persian cat, his yellow bulging eyes still beautifully intact, but his luxurious fur-coated ribcage crushed, cracked, tire-treaded? Why me with the shovel, the cardboard box, and duct tape preparing a body for burial? Tell me, why were you fried on a steel railing and not me shattered against a concrete abutment?

I still ask those questions while I lie on the edge of my mattress balancing myself on this side of safety, of sanity. I'm afraid that if I move, I may fall. I'm a woman with an emotional thermometer always in her mouth.

And so, Geoff, I'm asking for a consultation with a ghost. Isn't it time? Can I request the records now? Can I read them with the objectivity of a clinician, someone like a medical social worker, like me in my job turning the pages of patients' charts? Can I be ordinary again like one of the picnickers at Fort Foster on Gerrish Island in July of 1994 who abandoned a hamburger and potato chips to perform CPR on you and on Teddy?

Can I move from the intimate inside of our unfolding tragedy to the outside? Can I pass through a curtain like the white cotton one around Teddy? Let me set down my cup of cold tea and escape the shadowy intensive care unit; let me wander down the hospital corridors to the cafeteria and lift a plastic cup of pale tapioca in one hand, a plastic spoon in the other and then abandon them both. Let me flow like lukewarm tears past alcoves of grieving friends and relatives, and finally, make it to the emergency room exit. Let me reach the automatic doors that open in response to body weight, the doors that one can only move through if one survives. Have you watched me journey through the unpredictable stages of grief —a step forward, several steps backward, and then a stumble forward? Do you watch me now?

Will you allow me to move into the bright outdoors? Because I know I will shed memory, lose connection to the events. I'll find myself in the parking lot of York Hospital, and breathe in the warm steam of a July morning. Even in the shocked aftermath of sudden death, I'll stand beside the police detective and notice his attractive mustache. He'll open his wallet, expose his badge from the Town of Kittery, and I'll take notice of him as he extends a clipboard to me, as I grasp the pen he presses into my hand. But what if this time when I see the police report with the drawing of your body's awkward shape, what if it's just ink on paper?

Geoff, after this trip through the ER exit door, I'll be changed. No longer with every breath in and breath out will I see your hazel eyes peering out at the storm through the slit in the concrete bunker. I won't wonder if you saw the lightning as it streaked overhead, skipped other islands, other kayakers, and zipped and zapped its way to you. I won't see your hands grip the steel railing to ensure a completed electrical circuit.

On every sunny June/July/August day, I won't look up at the Maine sky and see the orange-red arrow that pierced the gravel gray sky and struck you. I won't hear the ping and pong of hailstones overhead on the metal roof or see the hundred thousand splashes off the pier. But instead I'll hold an armful of daisies, your favorite flowers, and toss them onto the surface of Kittery Bay and watch them float past me. I'll see only daisies falling in homage of love risked and ripped away—he loves me, he loves me not, he loves me. . . . He's dead.

Geoff, see me standing on the asphalt parking lot beside the courteous detective who is explaining to me that all accidents are initially considered crime scenes. It's just crazy; they just are.

I'm zoning out, escaping his words. I'm already busy converting the event, rewriting our family's tragedy. I'm looking at the smudged sketches of the bunker's concrete floor, blocking out images of splattered blood, and imagining/inventing/creating the myth that you had a second to face the rain and wind and that in that moment, you decided to take the first blast of lightning on yourself. As a widow, a mother, a writer, I want to believe in the myth and in you, that you were the hero who turned toward the east. I believe that it was not an accident that the first force of the bolt hit you.

I see the lightning finish with you before it passes to Teddy, our son who was turned away, who didn't see the streak of heat and sorrow. But what was unseen by Teddy was seen by you. That will be the lasting frame of memory for me: in a flash of fatherly impulse, you consciously took the heat for him. And when the crippled arrow entered the back of Teddy's head, before it randomly wriggled inside his body, it was partially spent. And by the time it skidded onto the cement floor beside his sneakered heels, it could only skitter. The lightning was powerless to kill Teddy because of you.

So when the EMTs arrived, took over CPR from the weary picnickers who were cramped up and exhausted pumping away at your heart, I understand that your vital organs except for your heart were utterly destroyed. In the ER, the IVs were useless, had nowhere to go. And your heart, your runner's heart, had nothing to spark and inevitably would run out of beats.

And later when your body lay upon the gurney, when I kissed your swollen cheek, you had been unconscious all the time after the accident. Isn't that right?

But even before arriving at the hospital, I was creating the story, the myth. On my way to the emergency room in the back seat of a speeding car at three in the morning, I developed the plot. If you died and Teddy survived, it would not be by chance or because of my prayers. Teddy would survive because you were a hero.

And when I read the medical and the police records, I'll be professional, I'll be detached. And I'll try to stick with the facts. But by then instead of a red arrow of lightning or scarlet splatters of blood, I'll see a red grosgrain ribbon like the page marker in a family Bible. It's that ribbon of love, not always just for you, but also for life itself that has inspired me while I've struggled with our family tragedy. I know the great Myth, but in my story, a father's instinct will be to sacrifice himself. Otherwise, I think the world would be upside down. Geoff, I'll bind our story with love and with courage; I'll lay a red ribbon on the title page. And in our myth, in our myth, the father will save his son.

PART II

―――

MY SEASON OF DEATH

o n e

MY SEASON OF DEATH

I have my own season of death—a husband, a father, a favorite aunt and uncle, and a sister-in-law. They died; they all died close together in time. Later, my mother-in-law. My mother. And then, my friend, David. Each death registered in intensity on my personal scale, each a shock, a smaller lightning strike on my lifeline. And each loss evoked memories of "the lightning accident." My life, my sons lives will forever be measured by our lives before and then after "the accident."

I DISCOVER THAT when I read obituaries, I react particularly to the phrase "he died peacefully." I sat by many deathbeds and none of my loved ones died peacefully. When I'm reading a page of obituaries and come across the repetition of the phrase, "he died peacefully, she died peacefully," I wonder if the Victorians are still influencing what we write about death. Are we still saying and writing what we think we ought to? I have a similar reaction to the obituaries that include "he died after a long courageous battle with cancer." No, of course, I don't doubt courage in the face of a terminal illness. But I wonder how cancer can be faced every moment with courage. What of the vulnerable moments when human resources are breached?

What of the stage in an illness when pain or fear humble every ounce of will? Is it fair to expect courage?

My father was brave and yet in his last moments, courage was not paramount. He didn't want to leave my mother alone. If I am pressed to describe my father's emotional state as he lay dying, it would be a heart full of regret.

And what about the others, my loved ones who died in my season of death? Not one of them died peacefully. My husband died first, in July of 1994; he died surprised. At forty-eight, he saw a white streak of lightning headed his way with shock and disbelief. Although he was an ardent student of Buddhism, he had no opportunity to compose himself into a meditative pose. He was dead in a flash. At least, I hope he was.

Then, a year later my father was dying, and my mother and I were the "family surrounding the loved one." My father was a model of dying well; he graciously thanked the nurse's aides for every small task they performed, even when their efforts caused him pain.

But after almost sixty years of marriage, nothing could prepare my mother for his death. I thought that she understood that once the morphine was increased to manage my father's pain, his breathing would fail, but although it was explained by a competent and sensitive nurse, my mother couldn't believe that my father had turned his back on her, that he had died and without her permission. It took a family friend, a male physician, to confirm that my father had moaned his last soft protests.

Later, my favorite uncle died. How may I describe his emotional state? Peaceful? No. More like absent. He had suffered from dementia for many years and was separated from my aunt in their nursing facility because of his mental deterioration. My mother and I just happened to be the ones sitting at his bedside when he neared death. When I saw the heightened sallowing of his skin, heard the shallow, irregular breathing, and noticed the distinctive tilt of his chin toward the ceiling or heaven, all signs of imminent death for me, I searched for my cousins.

I was deep into my role of deathbed sitter. I marched up to my oldest cousin and told him that he and his son, the oldest grandchild, should go to his father's bedside. It was pretty pushy of me as the youngest cousin, but I didn't think there was much time to spare. And I suppose I thought that in the years ahead my cousin would be glad he had been present at his father's actual death. Perhaps he is. Now, when I think back and especially because his father had for practicality's sake been gone for many years, I worry that I interrupted a life-affirming exchange between my cousins, the three brothers; maybe they needed the relief, even a little black humor, more than the stilted time by my uncle's bedside. Maybe I was out of line. Who knows? At the time, I thought I had a corner on death.

Later, my mother and I sat at my favorite aunt's deathbed wondering where my cousins were. I especially missed my cousin, Chris, my aunt's youngest. Why, I wondered, had my mother and I again inherited the role of being witnesses to a relative's last moments? My Aunt Anne was anxious. Maybe some of the anxiety was caused by visual hallucinations, a side effect of the morphine. But, no, she didn't die peacefully. Afterward my cousin Chris said he had left his mother's bedside so she could die without worrying about him, her baby. So there was no unbroken circle of family around my aunt's deathbed. And I was left still looking for a relative to die peacefully.

I was sitting at my aunt's bedside when my brother-in-law, Marshall, called me. I had promised. It was time. Two thousand miles away, Sarah, Geoff's older sister and my good friend, was dying of cancer. Her husband needed me to come. So without a break, I went from one deathbed to another.

Now, I was in a home, not in a hospital. My sister-in-law's

priority was for privacy as her body faced the last assault from ovarian cancer. She refused hospice care. I would miss hospice. My first role was making tea and toast and sitting quietly with Sarah so that my brother-in-law could rest. Later, I was by default responsible for whatever needed doing. . . .

Baby, their old golden retriever, had free rein of the house. The back door was always ajar in every kind of weather. I remember thinking there was no use in locking the door when Death had already found its victim. Baby was old, but he had a dog's knowledge that his mistress was dying. He lay sprawled beside her bed, half-hidden in the mussed sheets until she died, and then, he left.

And my sister-in-law, what was her state of mind? She was tiny, her body diminished by cancer's might. She made no pretensions of a courageous fight. She knew she was going to die, but she remained angry, even in a rage; she never wanted to go peacefully.

I'm still looking for a loved one who will die peacefully. Who are these people? Do they exist? Or do we feel compelled to make them up? What if we supported the sharing of what really happens? At death. Not always courageous, not always peaceful, not always a circle of loved ones, but often angry, anxious, absent, sad, or surprised.

What if we wrote about death just the way it is?

t w o

THE OLD SPANIEL

My Dad phoned last night.
"Girlie?" It's what he called me
though I was married with two sons.
"I've some sad news."
Bridget, the family dog since I was twelve,
had died. She'd crossed the room,
sat beside my father's leather chair;
her brown eyes locked on his blue;
she strained to do her trick, her only trick.
She extended her paw. . . .
Hundreds, thousands of times she shook his hand,
but this was for the last time.

"Thanks, Dad. Thanks for calling. I'm sorry."
"I love you, Girlie."
"I love you, Dad."

I felt the breathy whoosh of time
Like a warning shot across my bow;
I heard a loved body falling to the floor.
Then sometime in the unknown future,
I heard a beloved body falling,
too.

three

THE BEACHES

It is August in 1995 when I walk into my parents' den fitted out as a sickroom with a hospital bed. My father is in striped pajamas sitting in a leather recliner. "Where is your mother?" he asks.

"She's lying down," I say. I stayed with her until she fell asleep. My mother is in the master bedroom of my parents' high-rise condo. Several years previously when my father was first diagnosed with cancer, he initiated a move from their attractive home on a golf course at the edge of my hometown. They had lived surrounded by real prairie complete with rattlesnakes, jackrabbits, and meadowlarks. Moving had been a wise idea. Now my father is terminally ill, but he can take comfort in knowing that my mother is safely settled in a home close to friends and convenient to downtown Billings.

"Oh, it's good she's resting," my father says. "Maggie doesn't like going to the cancer center. It's hard on her."

"Yes," I say. "Dad, you must be tired. Don't you want to rest?"

"No, I'm wide awake," he says. "Besides, you and I don't have much of a chance to talk. Do we, Nance?"

"I'm sorry you're ill."

"I don't mind so much dying," my brave father says. "It's leaving your mother."

"Yes," I say. I do understand. My father lives in a traditional world where men protect women.

"I'm eighty-three. I've lived a long life." He pauses.

And I review in my mind the presidencies and world events he has lived through. He was excited about Kennedy being elected. Imagine a Catholic president. Then, saddened by the assassination. All that and so much more.

During the Depression, my father attended the University of Montana, but summers he lived on a cousin's sheep ranch near his hometown of Judith Gap. Over the years, he often teased, "I never want to eat mutton again." He served in the Navy during WWII, and when his ship ran short of vegetables, there were still bushels of Brussels sprouts. "I never want to eat another Brussels sprout," he joked. Every time he told the same stories, my mother and I laughed.

"NANCE," HE SAYS, "I haven't always been a good father."

"Oh yes, you have."

"I wish I'd been home when you were born and not away for so long."

"Me, too," I say, "but you couldn't help it. It was the war."

"Yes," my dad says. "It was the war. So terrible. For everyone." I nod. We are silent. "Recently," he says, "I've been having more memories of the war, especially about Iwo Jima. And about Japan—seeing the bombed cities."

"Oh," I say. It is new for my father to be talking about the war. I am used to his walking out when a movie about WWII comes on TV. "I think I'll go read my book," he has said so many times without any fuss.

"At Iwo Jima," he says, "the worst was having to direct the landing craft onto the beaches day after day."

I hold my breath, let him continue.

"Sometimes," he says, "the boats would stop short of the beaches and the marines, the men with their heavy packs and guns, would drown. And if the boats got to the beaches, most of the men would be shot or blown up before they could make any headway up the beaches."

"And you, Dad?"

"I was in a control boat a ways out in the water, but I had to keep directing wave after wave of men onto the beach, the beaches. Then, later, oversee the evacuation of the wounded."

"That's how you got the bronze star. Isn't it?"

"Mm-hmm."

I can tell he is seeing images from the war.

He asks, "Did you know it was supposed to be a silver star?"

"No." This is completely new information for me.

"On the sixth day of the battle, an Army colonel showed up. He was all gung-ho, waving to me, wanting his boat to go ahead of the others."

"So, what did you do?"

"I told him he'd have to wait his turn. Besides, what was an Army man doing in the middle of a Navy and Marine operation?" We laugh. "The colonel reminded me he had a star and asked for my name. 'Well, Lt. Bills,'" he said, "'I believe I have rank over you.'"

"So, what did you say?"

I said, "Bullshit! You're a damned fool. Why are you in such a hurry to die?"

"Oh, my gosh," I say. "Good for you, Dad."

"No. No, it wasn't so good for me. He didn't die. In fact, he filed a complaint against me. If I'd restrained myself, your father would have a silver star."

"I'm so sorry, Dad. What a bastard!"

"He sure was an S.O.B.," my dad says. We laugh. Together.

"Still, a bronze star is a great honor," I say. "And what a great story."

"Oh, you mustn't tell anyone. Your mother's still embarrassed about the whole thing. She was disappointed, wanted me to get promoted, to make the Navy a career. She took the whole thing mighty seriously."

"And you, Dad?" I ask.

"Well, I learned to be more careful about swearing." He smiles. "But, I'm a product of Judith Gap, Montana—the dusty plains, the open range. And sometimes, a man just has to swear."

"You look like you could rest, Dad."

"Yes," I'm tired." He tips his recliner back and closes his eyes.

"I love you, Dad," I whisper.

"Love you, Girlie."

On October of 1967, I'm at Lackland Air Force Base in San Antonio at an officers' training program. Frankly, I would have preferred the Navy, but my eyesight is poor so here I am, my father's daughter, his only child trying to fulfill the obligation of a son. He served in WWII, and so did his sister, my Aunt Mary, who was in the WAVES. The Vietnam War is my generation's war. So here I am.

"Thanks for coming along," Officer Trainee Major Jim Miller says to me. "You're going to make this really fun." I'm sitting up straight in the passenger seat of a jeep. We're wearing our winter blue uniforms according to regulation although the mid-October weather in south Texas is too warm for worsted wool. I'm perspiring both from the heat and my unease. Both of us have name tags across our chests and student insignia on our epaulets. I have two proud silver stripes on each shoulder; I'm an Officer Trainee Captain.

Jim and I have completed the more rigorous first six weeks of Air Force Officer Training School. Now in the second six weeks at Lackland Air Force Base, we enjoy OT rank and relatively more freedom. Still, I have no idea how Jim Miller got access to a jeep.

Soon, at the end of twelve weeks of training, almost all of the one thousand men and twenty-five women who began OTS will graduate and earn second lieutenant bars. Some, a few, will "wash out." In '67, the Vietnam War is heating up, and fresh officers are needed. We young lieutenants will go on to further training and then to God only knows where.

As the jeep speeds along on a Sunday morning, I say, "I've never been on this side of the base."

"I'm stationed over here. But your side has the better OT Club. That's why I was there last Saturday night." Jim, tall, confident and a good dancer, had bought me a couple of beers.

"I still don't understand why you wanted me to come along." I say. "Isn't it going to be awkward for the men?" *And for me,* I think. *I've never inspected men.*

"Oh, it'll be great fun showing up on a Sunday morning with you," he says.

As soon as we met last Saturday, Jim began bragging about doing inspections. That's when he hatched the idea and mockingly ordered me to accompany him. As an OT Major, conducting inspections is one of his prerogatives. He's keen to surprise someone.

Jim says he is weary of this man's boasting that he is from Scarsdale, New York, and from Greenwich Village. Jim says, "I'm looking forward to embarrassing this arrogant bastard and his precious platoon." Jim is going to be a pilot, and I can tell he believes pilots are superior to the rest of us.

"You're still game. Aren't you?" he asks.

"I suppose so," I say.

But I think, *I should never have agreed to come. I must have been a little drunk.* I glance at the lean, athletic man driving. I think, *He is much too smooth to really be my type.* I'm thinking, *I don't believe an inspection ought to be just a lark, or worse, to abuse one's rank.* But I don't say that.

Suddenly, we are at our destination, a low, long barracks built of concrete blocks. I step out of the jeep and slap Texas dust off the hem of my skirt. I straighten my hat, a hat I like a great deal; I keep its silver eagle insignia polished. The sun is harsh; I adjust my over-sized sunglasses and walk toward the barracks. I'm determined to be professional.

"Maybe you better wait outside," Jim says. "The men may not be dressed."

I wait, my two-inch heels sinking into the sandy soil; I do my best to look like I stand outside men's living quarters all the time. Within moments, I hear raised voices. In the midst of an argument I can't see but only imagine, I hear one loud, angry voice. A man emerges shouting at Jim, almost chasing him out of the barracks.

"Who do you think you are?" the man dressed in only box-er shorts and a white T-shirt asks Jim. "Why show up on a Sunday morning to inspect my men?!"

I can't help but peer at the entrance of the barracks, and I see men, lots of laughing men dressed only in what my father, my retired Naval officer father, calls skivvies; they are crowd-ing the doorway watching their obvious leader. This stranger, enraged at Jim's intrusion, yells, "Don't you know who my men are? They're graduate students." He continues after a pause, "The US Air Force is damn lucky to have them. If they hadn't been drafted two or three times by the Army, they'd still be in law or medical school." He stops just long enough to gulp a breath of hot Texas air. "Hell, if I hadn't been drafted four times by the Scarsdale Draft Board, I'd still be attending law school."

It is then that OT Major Geoffrey Green notices me, OT Capt. Bills, for the first time. "And who the hell is she?" he asks Jim. "And what is she doing here?"

And that's how I met my future husband, Geoff.

f i v e

HISTORY WITH GEOFF,
NUMBER 2, THE
LAST DANCE

On May of 1968, a banquet and dance at the Lowry Air Force Base Officers' Club in Denver, Colorado, offers a festive occasion for me and my fellow young officers. What a welcome relief from the demands of getting up for Armed Forces Intelligence School at 4:30 a.m. and the regimen of classes from 6:00 a.m. to noon and afternoons in the intelligence library doing homework.

"Let me get you a liqueur," Major Stratton says. Senior officers at our table have been buying drinks for Liz, my best friend, and me all night. After a heavy meal, many long speeches, I feel sleepy, but the major insists, "What would you like?"

"Oh," I say, "a Rusty Nail would be nice." I love the combination of scotch and Drambuie, the heat and the sweet.

Liz, my pretty and shrewd former roommate, nods at me from across the large round table, just senior officers—majors and colonels, and the two of us. She grew up in a military family as I did, and her glance says this flurry of attention is just for show and harmless. I sip from a tiny glass.

Then, 2nd Lt. Geoff Green is behind my chair asking me to be his partner in the last slow dance. Six feet tall with dark hair and hazel eyes and with the assurance of growing up in an affluent and cultured family, he exudes a confidence that I initially found offensive but came to experience as perversely attractive. I respect his upfront objection to the Vietnam War, enjoy his irreverence and humor, and am not immune to the charms of his beautiful skin, perfect teeth, and full and sensuous lips.

After Geoff and I met under such odd circumstances in the fall of 1967 at Lackland Air Force Base, I forgot about him for the most part. However, after we were commissioned as second lieutenants, both of us received orders to go to Lowry to attend lengthy training at Armed Forces Intelligence School, a prestigious specialty.

Instruction began with traditional subjects—geography and math. But later, our role related to the Vietnam War became clear; we were being prepared to brief pilots. Geoff and I had little contact until one month-long period of specialized training about choosing bombing targets. During those weeks of new realization and soul searching, we sat side by side and became friends. Shortly after, we became lovers.

THE MUSIC THE band is playing sounds old fashioned and sentimental, but it's still one of my favorites, "Save the Last Dance for Me." I am wearing the military's version of a feminine tuxedo. Designed by a French couturier, its white shirt has rows of ruffles on its front rather than pleats. I wear a trim skirt and a short fitted dress jacket, black with gold buttons. I even have two medals. In his dress uniform, Geoff with his flair for the absurd looks like a European count.

For the past several months, Geoff and I have lived in a large house on Clarkson Street not far from the Denver Zoo; we share it with three male officers, friends of Geoff's and now friends of mine. Mornings begin with the ten minutes Geoff and I are allotted in the single bathroom we all share. Geoff insists on playing "Cape-man," his version of a super hero. Naked with a towel flapping around him, he swoops down on me while I brush my teeth and shower. By the time he joins me in the claw-footed tub, I am dissolved in laughter. His performances are endearing; the youngest of four children, he makes fun out of everything.

Geoff and I have grown closer to one another, and as we face the uncertain future of our relationship—it seems inevitable that we will be separated, I wonder how we will manage without one another. I feel loved but vulnerable. This night of good food and dancing is bittersweet.

But despite the war and our anxiety, we smile as we sway to the familiar refrain of "Save the Last Dance for Me."

AS WE DRIVE home in Geoff's navy Mustang, he says, "I wish we could have sat together." He was at a table of Air Force second lieutenants and Navy lieutenants junior grade. I heard them having a great time—lots of laughter and off-color jokes. He says, "You should have been with us."

"I'd have had more fun," I say. "But I couldn't say no."

"At least we got to dance together." And we had.

As I drape my beautiful but tired uniform on the back of a chair in our bedroom, I say,

"I'm exhausted."

"So I guess no *Kama Sutra* for you tonight?" Geoff teases. In our early months together, we made good headway through his book until one afternoon when an oddball sexual position caused us to fall off the bed and laugh hysterically. Somehow, the book was pushed aside.

I feel woozy and only too happy to lie down on our lumpy bed side by side with Geoff.

"I really missed sitting with you," Geoff says. "Missed you." His voice trails off.

"Me too." I say. I think he must be half asleep. Moments pass, and I listen for his soft snores.

"Will you marry me?" he asks. "Marry me." I wonder if he is awake or dreaming.

I hesitate, almost sure he is asleep. If he is serious, I know we will face problems with my parents because he is Jewish. I wonder, *How will his parents feel about me? A Gentile marrying their nice Jewish boy.* But I love him so I whisper, "Yes."

The next morning, I'm the last one to join Geoff and our roommates downstairs; he's gone to a nearby deli for fresh bagels, smoked salmon, and cream cheese. During my shower in the claw-footed tub with the last of the house's hot water, I concluded that Geoff will have no memory of his sleepy proposal the previous night. I don't plan to mention it.

When the others abandon the kitchen, Geoff says, "I think we should sell one of our cars. We won't need them both."

Puzzled, I frown. He asks, "You do remember. Don't you? Last night? I asked you . . ."

"Yes," I interrupt him, "I do remember." *So he is serious,* I think. *What a lot of problems we will face—the Air Force, our parents.* But I say, "You're right. We won't need both cars."

"Why don't we keep yours," he says. "I like it."

"Okay," I say. I'm pleased for us to keep my Dodge Dart convertible.

Geoff embraces me and kisses the cream cheese off my lips. He tugs at my left hand and says, "We need to get you a ring."

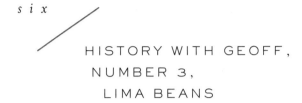

HISTORY WITH GEOFF,
NUMBER 3,
LIMA BEANS

A month after our June wedding, Geoff and I fly east to meet his extended family. The plane trip from Denver to LaGuardia is long, tiring; on the car ride to Scarsdale, I develop a headache; I am anxious about meeting my new husband's step-mother who did not come to our wedding. She has quite the reputation.

The houses on Stanhope Road are large, attractive. I don't know about *old money*, but I know money when I see it. Geoff's father's home is a white Colonial—stone foundation, green shutters, careful landscaping.

When the rental car, a new 1968 Ford Falcon, stops, I step onto the pea gravel of the driveway, but Geoff makes no move to get out so I duck my head back inside the car. I listen to the music on the radio, the last lines of the lyrics of Paul Simon's *Bridge over Troubled Waters*.

"Geoff," I ask, "You coming? I'm the one who should be dragging her feet."

Geoff emerges from the car and pulls a white cotton crewneck around his shoulders. "Wait till you meet my step-mother," he says. "She doesn't like to share my father. And she's full of nasty surprises.

"But your father's so nice." Geoff's father, Jacob, is charming, even courtly; he reminds me of Maurice Chevalier in *Gigi*, a movie I loved. "Your dad's been good to me, generous although he looks at me like I'm a prospective brood mare." We both laugh.

"Dad does like you," Geoff says. "He plans to treat you to theatre while we're here. Promise to be surprised." I nod. "He'll probably take us to his favorite restaurant, Lorenzo's—Italian, lots of waiters who genuflect to customers who leave big tips." He smiles. "The food is good. My favorite's the veal cannelloni, but let Dad order for you." Geoff gestures to the land adjacent to his father's back gardens. "That's the fifth fairway of the Oakridge Country Club."

Geoff hurries up a series of uneven garden steps so now, in my impractical Pappagallo shoes, I am the one who lags behind. "Come, look," Geoff calls pointing to a small pond. "These are my father's goldfish. He enjoys them and his tulip gardens." He waves at a corner of the property, and I imagine hundreds of spring bulbs blooming. We climb the back steps, and Geoff opens the door. Inside the closed entry, he holds out a hand to stop me. "Before we go in, there's something I've got to warn you about." I must look puzzled. "I'm serious. Be careful what you eat." I don't know what to say.

Inside the kitchen, Geoff draws me close to the refrigerator and opens its door. "Look at this," he says showing me a block of cheese heavy with green mold. Then from the very back, he pulls out a glass dish of cooked lima beans. "Probably a month old. Promise me you won't eat them."

"No, of course not."

We both respond to sounds from the upstairs. Geoff closes the refrigerator. I follow him, and we pass through the dining room; I admire a great, long mahogany table and pause in front of an impressive looking sideboard to examine a soup tureen with a gold monogram.

Geoff checks his watch. "Dad won't be home for a couple of hours." He whispers, "That means we're stuck with the cruel step-mother."

A disembodied voice calls out to us, "Geoff, is that you?"

Geoff pulls me by a hand through the formal living room to the front stairs. "Yes," he calls up the stairs. "It's Nancy and me."

"Oh, yes," the female voice says. "I'm resting. You know where the guest room is. Why don't you bring in your bags. Rest. Shower. Whatever. We'll have cocktails when your father gets home." A door above us closes.

"So?" I ask.

"That was our welcome," Geoff says. "I'll show you our room and bring in the suitcases."

After a nap that evolves into making love, after showering and dressing for dinner, Geoff and I go downstairs. We go through the living room to a garden room, and he makes us gin and tonics. We thumb through old copies of the *National Geographic* until his father arrives. He is welcoming, affectionate, and seems genuinely happy to see us.

When Geoff's step-mother joins us, we sit facing them— two gin and tonics, a bourbon on the rocks, and a vodka with a twist. When Geoff's step-mother withdraws to the kitchen, I follow, set the table as directed with china and silver and offer to help with the meal. In the kitchen, on the counter, I see two cans of vegetable soup and the glass container of old lima beans. Geoff's step-mother says she doesn't need help with dinner; it will be simple. Without preamble, she begins a litany of complaints—too bad it is the maid's day off, too bad the dining room at the country club is closed for renovations, too bad Geoff's father is too tired to go to a restaurant. Too bad.

After a second gin and tonic, I sit across from Geoff in the dining room, four of us sitting at a table for ten. His father sits in an armchair at one end of the venerable table and his step-mother at the opposite end nearest the kitchen; she carries in the first course of our meal, bowls of vegetable soup with the addition of the old lima beans. My efforts to warn Geoff non-verbally fail so he eats his soup including the dreaded lima beans. I try my best to avoid the beans leaving a dribble of them along the wide rim of my soup bowl and the rest at the bottom.

The next course is salad, usually safe, but Geoff's step-mother has scooped up the lima beans that I avoided in my soup and has sprinkled them over my salad. I can't believe it. Geoff sees the beans and smiles. Now, he says with no words, now, you know what my step-mother is like.

She says to me, "You need to eat your vegetables."

And so I do.

s e v e n

THE PROTEST

t's September of 1995. My mother and I are trying to create a normalcy we don't feel; our worlds are still reeling from my father's death five days ago.

I'm making a cup of Earl Gray for my mother. "Black?" I ask her from the kitchen of her high-rise condo. I know she takes her tea and coffee black.

"Yes, dear," my elderly mother calls out from the lanai with its floor to ceiling windows, with its wonderful views that she can no longer see. "You take milk. Don't you?"

I'm thinking, *I should have lied. I should have stretched whatever truth is and said to my dying father that yes, yes, Jules, a man I chose with less care than I would usually choose a head of lettuce, is marriage material.* I pour boiling hot water into two bone china tea cups. The one for my mother is pale green with flowers, a cup my father won in a bridge tournament long ago when he and my mother played together. When she could see. My cup is adorned with wild strawberries. I dip a Bigelow tea bag in and out managing to burn a forefinger. I sniff the milk carton and add milk to my cup.

"I'm coming," I call to my mother who sits straight-backed in a wicker chair at a round glass-topped table staring into space. I carry the cups of tea with care and then hurry to retrieve a plate of Pepperidge Farm shortbread cookies. I'm looking forward to their crumbly buttery taste although my appetite is generally poor. If only I had hesitated for a second; then, I would have spared my father the extra burden of leaving his only daughter without a man to protect her. Wasn't it bad enough that cancer was causing my father to abandon his blind wife?

My mother and I sit facing west, both of us warmed by the mid-afternoon sun. She still has a bit of peripheral vision; perhaps she can see the sparkle of my silver earrings or the bright pink of my polo shirt.

Growing up in Billings, Montana, I always felt oriented. My father often waved off to the south, toward the lazy, muddy Yellowstone River that wound between stands of cottonwoods and Russian olive trees and created the southern border of our world. To the north of my childhood home rose sandstone cliffs; above them, a broad tableland of sheep and cattle ranches with their arroyos and alkali creeks. To the east was the oil refinery that gave my hometown a distinctive odor that over time became familiar. And to the west rose the Beartooth Mountains, the foothills of the Rocky Mountains and a road, dangerous with its switchbacks, to the northeast entrance to Yellowstone Park.

I prefer the western view. I face it now. I could reach over and lift my father's binoculars, the large, heavy ones left over from "the war." With the help of those black Navy-issue binoculars that my father held scanning the horizon of the Pacific for the Japanese, I could scope out the early snow on the ski trails at Bridger Bowl, the ski resort where I learned to snowplow. If my father were here, that's what he would do. And so I can't.

"When are the boys coming?" my mother asks. I check my Swatch watch, but it has no hands, only a bee and a flower. I'm momentarily confused. "Never mind," she says.

"Their plane should be here soon," I say and study the

ragged sandstone cliffs that locals call the Rimrocks; the airport is atop "the Rims." My sons will be here soon. My cousins, who are flying in from D.C. and California, will arrive early this evening. In the morning, we will walk to the memorial service for my father at the Presbyterian Church next door. The doorbell rings. "Who?" I ask. It feels too soon for Simon and Teddy or for my cousin, Chris, and his brothers.

AFTER THE CATERER leaves, after the casseroles and salads are stashed in the refrigerator, I suggest to my mother that she try to rest even if she can't sleep. "Sometimes, I lie down just to rest," I say. I'm trying to model appropriate behavior just as I do with my patients.

"If you're tired, then you go rest," my mother says sharply. "I suppose someone will set the table. It's going to need all its leaves." She has outfoxed me again. I search for the table leaves and placemats. I distribute floral arrangements, lots of fragrant lilies, around the condo.

AFTER DINNER, I clear the table and begin the task of filling the hungry dishwasher.

"Mom," Teddy says entering the crowded kitchen. It's more than a year since the lightning accident killed his father, injured him, but he seems fine, no evidence of the balance problems he suffered from earlier. He's grown his brown curly hair long; the effect reminds me of Sunday school drawings of prophets from the Old Testament.

"Mom, you've got to come see this," Teddy says. I slam the dishwasher shut. He takes a handful of one of my sleeves in a fist and tugs me like he did when he was a child. He leads me out to the lanai where my mother and I sat drinking tea earlier.

Now, the sky is black except for a few blurred porch lights from nearby homes. Rain is pounding the giant panes of the windows in diagonal splats. "Listen," he says. "Do you hear it? The thunder?" We strain to hear the rumble of thunder beneath the murmur of voices in the condo. He slides the door between the lanai and the living room shut. I am certain now that what we are hearing is thunder. "It's my dad," he says. "The thunder is Dad."

I am puzzled. Why is Teddy envisioning his father as thunder? What does it mean? Is it okay? Is it therapeutic? Maybe. It means that his dad hasn't disappeared. "It's getting louder." That's all I know to say.

Simon enters the porch just as the lightning begins with flashes and bursts around us. The unpredictable streaks are frightening, but I am mesmerized as I was when I grew up here and saw a tornado. "Look," I said to my father. "Look," was all I could say.

The thunder throttles my parents' tall high-rise and shakes the concrete floor of the lanai; I wish for the first time that my mother lived on a lower floor. The scene indoors, the quasi-normal image of my mother seated in a coral chair chatting with my cousin, Lee Ann, is in stark contrast with the vast black void that surrounds me and my sons. Lightning suddenly illuminates the Rimrocks; then its absence plunges them into darkness. The Rimrocks, darkness, alternating again and again.

"The thunder. It's Dad's voice," Teddy tells Simon. "He's protesting Grandpa's entry into heaven."

I catch Simon's eyes. I know Simon. He doesn't believe in heaven. Or hell. Teddy may believe that everything happens for a purpose, but Simon believes that we live in a world of chaos and chance. I'm worried that he's not going to buy the idea of the thunder being his father's voice. "Well," he says to Teddy, "Dad was no fan of either Grandma or Grandpa." He looks at me for help. "They didn't go to your wedding. Did they, Mom?"

"No, they didn't. I suppose your dad would never have forgotten that." And I haven't been able to forget that more than twenty-five years ago when Geoff and I were married in a garden in Denver, my parents were not present at our wedding. Because Geoff's family was Jewish. No wonder Geoff has the voice of thunder and is protesting.

e i g h t

BABY IN THE
BACK ROOM

I n October of 1997, three years after Geoff's death, I receive a
call from my brother-in-law, Marshall. "You said you would
come," he says. "And we need you now." His voice cracks. "Can
you come?"

"Do you have hospice?" I ask. They must; Sarah, my husband's older sister, is in the last stages of ovarian cancer.

"Sarah doesn't want strangers coming in," Marshall says.
"She's determined to keep everyone away." And I understand
that she will not want her mother visiting, her difficult mother. But surely her sister and her friends. And nursing care. "I
haven't told her that I'm calling you," he says. "But I can't manage any longer on my own."

"I'll come," I say although I would have liked to have gone
home to New Hampshire first. I'm in Montana staying with
my mother whose only sister has just died.

But I fly to Newark, New Jersey, rent a car, and drive to
North Plainfield. Sarah and Marshall's home is a big rambling
Dutch Colonial surrounded by tall maples and oaks. I prepare
myself to enter a household where the priorities are food and
dogs. And even though I know Sarah is gravely ill, I half expect to find her with Marshall sipping coffee, eating bagels,
and reading *The New York Times* in their sunny breakfast

room with Baby, their elderly golden retriever, at their feet. As I pull my rolling suitcase over the cracks of the narrow walkway to the back door, I smell moldy earth. The screen door is ajar, a sight that strikes me as neglect rather than welcome. "Come in, come in," Marshall says. I reach back to close the screen, but he says, "No, no, just leave it open. Baby needs to get in and out on her own." The elderly dog is noisily drinking from her water dish, but she turns to acknowledge me; her muzzle is flecked with white; her tail is speckled with bits of yellow and orange leaves.

"Poor old girl," he says patting her head.

I hand over my suitcase and reach up and give Marshall a kiss on the gray stubble on his cheek. He is in the midst of unpacking grocery bags. "Let me help," I say.

"Just anywhere," he says. But the refrigerator is stuffed full, and the counters are overflowing. I am stymied about where to put anything. When I attempt to enter the pantry, I stumble over a carton of canned dog food and yelp. "You can see what it's like," he says waving a helpless hand at the kitchen.

"How's Sarah?" I ask. Marshall answers with a shake of his head. He looks grizzled; even his complexion looks gray.

"Just checked her," he says pointing overhead to indicate the back bedroom, the one at the end of the second floor hallway. "She's sleeping."

"Shall I go to sit with her? I ask. "Now?"

"First have some tea and toast," Marshall says. "There's marmalade. I got fresh butter. That," he says pointing at a crumb-covered cube on a china saucer, "is rancid." He makes no effort to scrape it into the trash.

"You look exhausted," I say.

"I am. Going up to sleep," he says. "Can you stay with her? For six hours?" It's not so much a question as an instruction. "Then wake me."

"All right," I say. "What do I do?"

"If she wakes up, try to get some water in her. And give her a morphine tablet." He pauses. "No, give her two. With any luck, she'll go back to sleep." He turns away. I hear him rolling my suitcase in from the back hallway and a series of grunts as he carries it up the stairs. From the landing, I hear his muffled voice, "You'll be in the front bedroom." There is a silence and then he adds, "Oh, you'll have to change her."

I PROMISED I would come to help when Sarah got really ill. She and Marshall were so good to me when Geoff died. It's been too long since I've seen her. She put me off. "This isn't a good time," she said several times and months went by. At first, she delayed resigning from her social work job; then she spent her last bits of strength caring for private patients, patients she saw here in her office at the front of this big old house.

One of the last times I saw Sarah was in Connecticut at Teddy's wedding; she attended the service, even went to the reception but left early. Over time she had become progressively weaker and not able to enjoy meals out, one of her dependable pleasures.

I munch on a piece of toast generously buttered and slathered with marmalade. *So, I think, this is what it all comes down to—Sarah dying in the back bedroom, Marshall sleeping, and me eating toast, stunned that she is leaving us.* I stand in front of the kitchen sink looking out over the backyard; a maple tree dwarfs the house, casts its ragged shadow on us.

I carry my mug of tea up the stairs kicking idly at dead leaves; I suppose Baby carried them in on her fur. At the doorway of the front bedroom, I flick on the light switch and glance inside. Marshall has set my suitcase near a sofa bed. I walk through to the French doors and open them letting a welcome draft of mild air enter the stuffy room.

Studying the space where I will sleep, my attention is drawn to the bookcase. On the middle shelf, a card is prominently displayed: a dog sled is being drawn by pairs of huskies across an Arctic scene. I pick it up. Marshall has drawn a figure on the sled and written "SARAH" beside it. And he has printed the names of their deceased dogs beside the sled dogs; one name is that of the yapping cocker spaniel who was blinded in one eye and another is the name of the hyper-active Airedale responsible for the injury. The card with its tender notations portrays a sled carrying Sarah, drawn by her beloved dogs, headed toward heaven. Returning the card carefully to its place of honor, I exhale.

Taking a sip of strong Earl Gray with milk, I head down the hallway to the back bedroom. As I pause in the doorway, I see Baby's limbs splayed out across the bare hardwood floor. Her head is hidden under a rumple of coverlet hanging from the bed, but I can see the rest of her furry body.

I whisper, "It's okay, Baby. It's me." As she shifts her weight, a flag of blond tail waves, and I hear a familiar thump, thump, thump against a radiator.

The room is small and square barely lit by wall sconces; the lace curtains on two small-paned windows hang limp. I sniff the mix of unwashed dog and disinfectant in the heated air and take two small experimental steps past the threshold. Sarah is sleeping. *Thank Heavens,* I think relieved.

LAST SPRING WHEN I visited, I slept in this rarely used bedroom and wakened to look at the morning glories on the wallpaper. A May breeze brushed along my bare arms, and I pulled a patchwork quilt up to warm myself. Today, I can see the same quilt folded on a shelf in the bedroom's closet.

Now, a gray steel hospital bed dominates this room where Sarah lies curled on her side, her size and shape obscured by a coarse, striped blanket. The head of the bed is raised, and her body slumps toward the foot. Sighing involuntarily, I stare at her tiny frame, at her skull covered in short dark fuzz.

I tiptoe into the room, but Sarah awakens, her eyes widen. "Why are you here?" she asks me.

"Where else would I be?" I answer. It turns out to be the right response. She closes her eyes and is immediately asleep. I study the room, take in the vial of morphine tablets, the glass of water with a straw, the boxes of adult-sized paper diapers. I have volunteered for this duty and am committed to doing my best. As I sit down in an upholstered chair, Baby's large head drops to the floorboards with a soft bump. I sip my tea.

On a February morning in 2001, I am on the telephone with Bitsy, Geoff's brother's wife, in New York City, when she interrupts our conversation. She says, "I've got a call waiting. I think it's the hospital. Let me phone you right back." And I know, the way one does. The hospital is calling because Iris, my mother-in-law, is dead. I phone Teddy in Connecticut.

"Your grandmother's dying," I say. "She may be dead already. I'll call back when I have more news." Teddy is a veteran of death; he was only twenty when his dad died. Before that, his beloved horse, Gentle to Market, the gray thoroughbred he called Mark, suffered from colic and died when he was only fifteen. And he's lost his Aunt Sarah and his Grandpa John. A lot of losses.

Moments later, the phone rings again. "She just died," Bitsy says. "The doctor was prepping her for surgery. And she died." She tells me more details that wash over me—a fall, a broken hip, hemorrhaging, hemorrhaging. And dead.

"I'm so sorry," I say to Bitsy and then to Yale, my brother-in-law, Geoff's older brother. Iris was eighty-nine.

For the twenty-six years I was married to Geoff, I was Iris's daughter-in-law. When Geoff died, I wondered if Iris was still my mother-in-law. I wasn't sure. But I continued to send birthday cards and gifts. I stopped sending Mother's Day cards, but I kept the phone number of her local florist handy.

Iris was a difficult woman to have as a mother-in-law. Frankly, she was a demanding and oppressive woman. Bright. Educated at Hunter College in New York City. She earned a doctorate at Columbia University while my Geoff was in grade school. Her four children agreed unanimously that graduate school was responsible for the disintegration of their parents' marriage. Iris was a liberated woman before it was fashionable. She liberated herself from her marriage and her role of active mother when my Geoff was ten.

Iris's apartment in New York City was sophisticated and luxurious. Her country home with her second husband near the New York border with Connecticut was attractive and comfortable; the grounds included a sauna house and a swimmable pond with an island. Wherever she lived, she always knew the best restaurants, the current art museum shows, and the most favorably reviewed plays, movies, and nonfiction books. She was conversant in multiple languages, and by the time she died, she had traveled all over the world. She had even ridden a camel in Egypt.

On a last cruise around the world, somewhere near the Philippines, Iris became seriously ill. The ship's doctor made the diagnosis of ovarian cancer and sent her home. The cancer was already well-advanced.

During Iris's last illness, I went to visit her every several months. I drove from Maine to the graduated care facility in Massachusetts where she lived among other affluent and educated elderly residents. I kept the visits short. I wished that Iris and I had a better relationship because I knew it was just a matter of time.

During my last visit, she was in her facility's health center. Lying on a hospital bed, her distended abdomen was evidence of her incurable cancer. As I was leaving, I leaned forward to kiss her on her cheek. "No," she said pulling away. "My immunity, the chemo." But she and I knew she had a difficult time with closeness. Kindness was intolerable. Somewhere in her past, there were explanations, secrets.

Geoff, my psychologist-husband, had been fascinated with his mother's family history. He theorized that when Iris had been an infant and a child, her mother had abandoned her to the care of a young, illiterate black maid. He was endlessly intrigued by what had occurred while his grandmother had carried on an affair with Orthodox Judaism and a rabbi.

SO AFTER A long struggle with cancer, Iris is finally dead. In the dim light of early morning, she stumbled out of bed and fell. Her hipbone cracked, and the arteries around the joint burst. And she hemorrhaged.

"Just as well," Yale says. Although it is a cruel thing to say, I have to agree. Iris has been battling ovarian cancer for three years. If she had survived, the next several months would have been only more grim. She put up a formidable battle. I'm not sure if she was fighting to live or fighting not to die. But she had plowed through abdominal surgery, chemotherapy, more surgery, more chemo. She was tough. But she knew, we all knew, she was going down.

MY LAST CONTACT with Iris was a note card, a "thinking of you" card; I enclosed a photograph of her deceased son, my Geoff. On one of Teddy's visits to Maine, he and I took our favorite photo of his dad to the local drug store and made a digital enlargement. We placed a picture of Geoff dressed in canvas shorts and a plaid flannel shirt face down on the copier.

We adjusted the cropping mechanism until the image of his dad leaping over a mountain stream was centered, until his muscular legs and leather hiking boots were of equal distance from each shore, until his feet were suspended in airy perfection above boulders and rushing water. When I nodded, Teddy pushed the button. A glossy enlargement dropped into the slot. We agreed that the other-worldly photo captured just what we wanted to express.

"Do you think Grandma Iris will understand why we're sending the picture?" Teddy asked me.

"I don't know," I said. I didn't think so, but that didn't mean we shouldn't send it.

Iris was a difficult person. In 1994, when I had called her with the news that Geoff had been killed by lightning, it was seven in the morning. After I shared the bad news, she demanded, "Did you have to wake me up in the middle of the night? Couldn't you have waited?" Geoff had died at 3:50 a.m. so I had already waited to call. I had waited as long as I thought I should, as long as I could to call a mother.

Despite everything that had happened, I persisted in wanting to wake Iris up. I still worried she had slept through one of the most important parts of her life. Perhaps if she saw the photo of Geoff, the mystical photo, she would understand that Geoff was waiting for her, waiting suspended in limbo.

Perhaps, the mother of my late husband, the troublesome and troubled Iris, would finally discover her youngest child.

I hoped so.

TEDDY'S HISTORY,
GENTLE TO MARKET

The spring of 1989 is muddy in New Hampshire. Both Margaret, Teddy's horse trainer, and I are dressed in riding clothes—boots, britches and quilted jackets; we stand in her chilly office at the horse barn south of Deerfield. I've been at her farm since mid-morning when I arrived for a lesson. By then, Margaret had called the vet who had come to the barn. Margaret had tried to carry on as usual until it became clear that Teddy's horse, Gentle to Market, was not responding to the prescribed medical treatment. That's when Margaret and I agreed that I needed to share our troubling news with Teddy.

"I need to pick Teddy up early," I say into the phone. I don't have time to explain my reasons to the secretary at my son's day school in Manchester. Margaret nods at me. "Please get him out of class. Tell him to meet me at our usual place."

"What shall I record as the reason you are taking him out of school?" the voice asks.

"A family emergency." I put the phone down on its hook without saying goodbye. The last of the spring snow is gone; the traffic on the back roads shouldn't be bad, but still it's a good thirty minutes to get to Teddy.

⌁

HE'S WAITING FOR me with his heavy backpack in one hand, a lacrosse stick in the other. As I brake the car, he opens the rear door and hefts his gear onto the back seat. I lean over to unlock the passenger door, and he's inside with me. I step on the gas pedal of our family's Subaru station wagon and head east.

"What's up?" Teddy asks. "How come you're picking me up early?"

All the way from the barn, I have promised myself that I will tell Teddy the bad news one bit at a time. He's only fifteen. Although his dad and I and Simon, his older brother who is away at college, are in the habit of treating him like an adult, he's only fifteen. But now that I'm in the car with him, I have the impulse to tell him everything in one big exhalation. It's an impulse I intend to fight.

"Bad news," I say glancing over at his suddenly serious face. "Prepare yourself for bad news."

My concentration is split between driving as fast as I can safely manage and sharing upsetting news to the best of my ability. "It's Mark," I say. Mark is our family's nickname for Gentle to Market, Teddy's six-year-old gray thoroughbred. As the car escapes suburban traffic and enters farmland, I watch the speedometer climb. I think, *God, I would like to be doing any-thing else but this.* Teddy loves his horse; they have been a team for the last year; Gentle to Market is true to his name—a smooth ride, a sweet temperament, and a delight to see in motion. Mark is Teddy's best friend.

"What's wrong?" Teddy asks.

"Colic."

"Colic?" he asks.

"Yeah," I say. Margaret found Mark down in his stall this morning. A horse doesn't usually lie down; they even sleep standing up; lying down is a bad sign. Mark had kicked boards out of the sides of his stall. The poor beast was in excruciating pain. Colic, a twisting of the intestines, is painful for horses and dangerous.

"So Margaret called Dr. Anderson?" he asks.

I nod in assent. Dr. Anderson is the local large animal veterinarian; Teddy knows him, has helped him when the vet has come to the barn. I have visions of Teddy becoming a veterinarian. Maybe Teddy has them, too. "So?" Teddy asks me leaning across the car to look me in the eye.

The standard treatment for colic is to thread a tube down the throat of a horse and to pour quarts of mineral oil into the stomach; usually this resolves the blockage in the animal's insides. The horse is walked until the problem rights itself. Teddy is familiar with the problem, one that can most often be avoided if horses are walked after strenuous exercise, walked until their bodies cool.

"Is it my fault?" he asks me.

"Oh, no," I say. "No! You didn't do anything wrong." I hold a hand up in the space between us. I don't want my son feeling guilty. After our lesson in the cold indoor arena last night, I walked my horse, Lady, and he walked Mark around and around, not the most enjoyable part of riding. Margaret had worked Teddy and Mark hard; both were sweating, but Teddy had cooled his horse just the way he had been taught. I say, "I even made you walk him around a couple of extra times." I am relieved that I did. In this moment, I'm thankful for my caution.

"Mark didn't respond," I say. I hate delivering this news to Teddy. "Mark didn't get better."

"No?" he asks.

"No," I say. We are both silent.

"Teddy, Dr. Anderson recommended that Mark go to a specialist in Lee." As I share this news, I picture the vet's pickup hauling a shiny silver horse trailer and making good progress along Route 4. "So I called your dad. He agreed. Mark is on his way. He should be there by now."

"Another vet? A specialist?" Teddy asks.

"Mm-hmm," I murmur. We are both silent as I speed up the Subaru and make good time until we reach Candia. Then I have to slow down through what locals know is a speed trap. As we go down the hill and through the small village, I say, "I'm sorry." It seems a pitiful thing to offer.

"I know, Mom," he says. We both love riding. We started by learning on two of the barn horses—Mickey and Stubby; we are both thrilled to have our own horses. My mare, High Country Lady, is an attractive paint, but no match for Mark's classy looks. Margaret thinks Teddy's natural talent and Mark's elegant presentation make them a promising team for hunter class competitions. She has dreams for them.

"Your dad is going to meet us at the barn," I say. "Meanwhile, Margaret is in touch with the vet in Lee." I pause. Now, I must share what feels like the most alarming news. I look across at my son to see how he is doing. "Teddy, your dad had to give permission for Mark to have surgery if necessary."

Teddy doesn't make a sound.

Passing Margaret's house and pond, I slow down to turn onto the muddy, rutted road to the barn; we're almost there. I take in a big breath. Lady with her distinctive white blaze trots in the small paddock. I ignore her; to take pleasure in her movement, her intact beauty, seems like a betrayal in this moment. I pull the Subaru up to the barn door; Teddy and I exit in one motion.

As we walk up the main aisle, my body responds to the familiar smells of the barn—horse manure, hay and tanned leather; they are a comfort. I sniff the cold air for the fragrance of alfalfa. I imagine a cube of alfalfa in my hand, and a horse's velvety lips and moist nostrils snuffling my palm for a treat. As we pass Mark's stall, nothing appears amiss; there is no sign of the beloved horse's agony.

Margaret, a surrogate mother to my son, comes out of her office. "I'm so sorry, Teddy," she says and holds her arms out wide. Her embrace says these moments of acute worry are part of owning horses, riding horses, loving horses. We are silent as we file into her office. "Your dad's on his way. He should be here any minute." As soon as we sit down, she reaches out a hand and pats Teddy's forearm. "Teddy," she says, "the vet in Lee has decided to proceed with exploratory surgery."

"Oh," Teddy says. I move my chair closer to his. The office feels cold.

"The vet will call as soon as she opens him up." Regretting her frankness, she says, ". . . as soon as she knows anything." We sit quietly struggling not to imagine the scene.

After a long interval, I hear Geoff's voice. Margaret goes to the doorway and calls out to him. He enters and reaches down to kiss me. The brush of his soft beard and mustache against my cheek are a fleeting comfort. He claps Teddy on the back. "Sorry, kid," he says. "I told the vet to do everything she can to save Mark." He asks Margaret, "So the horse is in surgery?"

"Yes," we three say. I imagine the body of the dappled gray horse under anesthesia, his belly open. We wait for the vet to call. We agree that Margaret will take the call because she is the most knowledgeable about horses.

When the phone rings, I listen to Margaret's noncommittal replies—"Yes . . . of course . . . no . . . all right . . . okay." Then she says to Teddy, "Why don't you come with me. Let your parents talk to the vet."

While Geoff listens to the vet, he frowns and shakes his head. I see tears well up in his eyes. "I understand," he says. "You had better talk with Teddy's mother."

I should be prepared for the extent of the bad news, but still it comes as a shock. The vet has discovered a congenital defect; she is surprised that the beautiful horse has lived as long as he has. His condition would require major surgery, the removal of most of the small and large intestines that are necrotic, but it is her expert opinion that after surgery, Mark would not receive enough nutrition to thrive. She concludes that Mark would die a slow death from starvation. When I press her for answers, she is clear. She doesn't believe Mark could return to health. Teddy would never be able to ride him. Confident in her conclusions, her recommendation is that Mark be put down.

"May we have a few minutes to talk?" I ask this vet in Lee whom I don't know but who is both forthright and kind. "We'll call you back," I say, "in just a few minutes."

I stand and walk to Geoff. We are both crying. "Poor Teddy," I say. "He loves Mark so much." We hold on to one another. I ask my husband, "How will Teddy ever forgive us for putting his horse down?"

"I think he needs to talk to the vet," Geoff says. "Mark is his horse. It needs to be his decision."

"What a burden for him," I say. "He's just a boy."

"He's always been older than his years. Wiser." Geoff says.

"He'll want to know everything," I say. I hate to think of Teddy hearing all the details I've listened to. But maybe Geoff is right. Maybe it's for the best.

"I'll tell him that we'll abide by his decision," Geoff says.

"But what if he wants to keep Mark alive? No matter what?"

"He won't," Geoff says. "You'll see."

⌒᧿⌒

I MAKE ROOM for Teddy to sit next to the phone. He listens to the vet. Asks questions. Listens. "Yes," he says. "I understand. Hold on, please." He sets the phone's receiver down on the desk. He looks at his dad, at Margaret, and at me. "I'll tell the vet to put Mark down on one condition," he says.

"What?" we ask. "Anything you want," we say in unison.

"I want Mark buried here at the farm," Teddy says. Margaret nods. She will have to think of where. Geoff nods. He must think of how, how to get a thousand pound dead and stiff horse to the farm. My son looks at me.

"Of course," I say. His request seems so modest given his sacrifice. "But," I say, "Will you agree not to be here." I look through the walls of the barn and imagine a front loader carrying a gray horse in a strange funeral procession down the lane past the outdoor riding arena to an open field. Sometime in the future, I imagine a granite marker—GENTLE TO MARKET, Beloved Friend.

"Teddy," I ask, "Will you agree not to be here when Mark is buried? I want you to remember him when he was alive."

"I agree," my Teddy says. He raises the phone.

e l e v e n

PLANTING IRIS

On a Sunday afternoon in May of 2001, we, the Green family, have gathered in the new part of the Riverside Cemetery in Cape Elizabeth, Maine, for a graveside service. We, the family, stand in an uneven circle around a small open grave.

Yale, my late husband's older brother, asks, "Anyone else? More prayers? More poems?"

I have a prayer with me, but I shake my head along with the others. "No, no," we murmur." Across the circle, my sons, Simon and Teddy, shoot a certain look at me. Soon, their Grandma Iris who died in March of cancer will be underground. And it will be a relief.

Yale, one of Iris's two surviving children, bends forward, grasps the urn, and raises it from its bed of stiff plastic grass. He shows the urn around the circle; gold, green, and red swirls undulate around the curvaceous vase giving the illusion of fiercely swimming fish.

One of us exclaims, "Beautiful!" Another says, "Just like Iris." I know one true thing: Iris would have loved our rapt attention.

Despite the urn's beauty, we silently express our various thoughts, *"Pretentious. A useless expense. No respectable New Englander would have it!"*

"I chose it," Lily, Iris's older daughter, announces with pride. "It's cloisonné."

"How do you say it?" someone asks. Lily corrects the ignorance, "Cloisonné with an accent." My sons and I roll our collective eyes.

The family muses that Lily's choice of urn, its colorful enamel on metal, is her effort to package her mother in safety, in comfort, even in elegance for the trip to wherever women like Iris go. None of us can be certain.

Lily recalls her mother's attributes: "She was a psychoanalyst, a world traveler, an avid reader, a museum buff, a linguist of six languages, a proud New Yorker, a cultured, well-educated, liberal feminist. And a film critic." Lily pauses. "My mother was a critic generally." And we laugh as we are meant to.

I add silently, *my mother-in-law was a royal pain in the ass.* My late husband, Iris's youngest, believed that she was a toxic narcissist.

To catch our attention, Yale clutches the urn dramatically to his chest. With an expression of childlike willfulness, he feigns that he will drop the urn. "Oh. Ohhh," he utters staggering this way, then that.

"Stop it," Lily commands as if to a troublesome, stuttering little brother. "Don't you dare drop that urn."

Yale smiles a grin of revenge.

"No. No, for God's sake, Yale," Lily cries. "Do you know what it cost?"

"Just teasing," Yale says.

Maybe we need the comic relief.

Then not finished with being naughty, Yale lowers the urn to the eye level of the great-grandchildren. He calls to the sweetly dressed boy and girl. "Look. Look," he says. "This is your Great-Grandma Iris. This is the last time you'll see her." He holds the urn with its mysterious contents out to little Rose and Frankie. "Say goodbye to her." The children look puzzled, also skeptical.

"Give it up, Yale," Lily says.

Hopefully refocused on his somber role, Yale returns his attention to his task. We, the family, nod encouragement. We offer silent wishes for the burial to proceed. Please, we pray, let Yale end his antics. Please let him lower the showy urn into the empty cubic foot of space beside the plastic grass. Soon, we silently pray. Let it be soon, rhyming with swoon.

But it is not to be. A surprise comes as Yale raises the urn. As he fully extends his arms, he sees a paper fluttering from the urn's bottom. He squints and begins to read, but then exclaims, "I'll be God-damned. These ashes aren't mother's."

"It should say Dr. Iris Gruen," Lily says. Iris went by the name of her second husband.

"I know what it should say," Yale says. "I swear, Lily, the label says the ashes belong to some other lady."

"Who? Who?" We, the family, ask like owls.

"Miriam Weiss. These are the ashes of Miriam Weiss."

We, the family, are shocked by the dawning idea that the ashes in the urn may not be Iris's. And we ask ourselves, "Who was Miriam Weiss?"

For a moment, Yale and Lily are speechless. Then, she demands, "Let me look."

He upends the urn. She reads the label, "The remains of Miriam Weiss."

Yale returns the urn to its "grass." He waves the family away saying, "We need some time."

Our family circle disperses. Lowering our glances, we try to mute our curiosity. We do our best to ignore Lily's frantic fumbling in her purse. We try not to hear her ask, "Where's my damn cell phone?" We try to block out her exclamation, "Mr. Burroughs Waterstone, the Director of the Waterstone Funeral

Home in Needham, Massachusetts, is going to wish he was dead!"

We, the family, think that it's Sunday. In Maine, nothing much happens on Sundays. We wonder who Lily will be able to reach.

Yale says, "Well, family, it looks like this is going to take some time."

The spring breeze halts; the young afternoon feels oddly still. In the newly opened part of the cemetery, we are surrounded by spindly trees, a sparse scattering of new graves. We, the family, ponder the absurd, not only the most recent madness, but all of life's and death's absurdities.

Marshall, my brother by marriage, sits down cross-legged on the cemetery's grass. His laughter begins like bath bubbles but bursts into uncontrollable hysteria. As he rolls on the grass and dandelions, he gives voice to our thoughts, "This is crazy. Crazy."

The spectacle frightens little Rose. "Get up, Great Uncle Marshall," she says. "You'll get your clothes all dirty."

He stands brushing strands of grass from his tweed jacket and twill pants. He pats Rose's head to comfort her. "It will be all right," he says, not believing a word of it.

A cell phone beeps. "It's the director," Lily whispers to Yale. "He says we have the right ashes. If we want to know for sure, there's a metal ID tag in every urn."

Yale tries hard to twist the top. "No way," he says. Tell him it's on too tight."

"The director says we could postpone the service, bring the urn to them." Lily says, "Yes, Mr. Waterstone," she says into the phone, "we'll talk it over and get back to you. Goodbye."

The siblings consider their options: Lily says, "I'm not driving to Massachusetts then back to Cape Elizabeth." And Yale says, "Well, I'm certainly not going to drive to the City and back here either. Why would I?!"

Embarrassed for Lily and Yale, we wander off; some read names on gravestones, others hunt for candy bars in glove compartments. I walk down the hill to the old part of the cemetery; there the symmetry of the rows, the lichen on aged gravestones, and the dark pairs of dwarf spruces satisfy my need for order.

At the gravestone of my late husband, Iris's youngest child of four, I whisper, "Geoff, you wouldn't believe what's going on up the hill. Be glad you're down here." I survey his view of a simple white chapel and the graceful marsh. I think that he must get a good view of the sunset, but quickly dismiss my thoughts as foolishness.

I cross the gravel road to Sarah's gravestone. "We're trying to bury your mother," I tell her. "She's as much trouble dead as she was alive." I know what Sarah would say—"Just keep her far, far away from me."

"Mom," Simon and Teddy call out running down the hill to me. "They say they're ready. They want us."

We, the family, once again fall into our uneven circle.

Yale speaks, "Thank you for your patience. After speaking with the funeral home . . ."

Lily breaks in, "Yale and I have decided the ashes in the urn are mother's. We'll proceed with the burial."

"A prayer might help," Yale says. "Anybody? An appropriate prayer?" What an unexpected request! But I do have an all-purpose prayer. I raise my hand. "Not too long," Yale cautions.

I nod. I pass a copy to Simon and Teddy, and we read the responsive prayer.

In the rising of the sun and in its going down,
we remember them.
In the blowing of the wind and in the chill of winter,
we remember them.

In the opening of buds and in the rebirth of spring,
we remember them.

In the blueness of the sky and in the warmth of summer,
we remember them.

In the rustling of leaves and in the beauty of autumn,
we remember them.

In the beginning of the year and when it ends,
we remember them.

When we are weary and in need of strength,
we remember them.

When we are lost and sick at heart, we remember them.

When we have joys we yearn to share, we remember
them.

So long as we live, they too shall live, for they are now a
part of us, as we remember them.

—Roland B. Gittlesohn,
Singing the Living Tradition, Beacon Press, Boston,
The Unitarian Universalist Association, 1993, #720.

The prayer works wonders.

Yale kneels on the "grass" and places the urn in the grave.
He speaks to Lily *sotto voce,* "Let's get out of here before anything else happens." They run to their cars in a rush. They
wave. Leave with a spit of gravel.

We, the family members, hug and kiss. We conclude that
"Yes. Yes, it is a big relief. Either Iris or Miriam has been buried."

After Lily and Yale and all the rest of the family had
gone home, I thought we, the Green family, had done
a good job of getting Iris into the ground. I thought the saga
was over.

But three days later, I have news I want to share with Teddy. I call from my car.

"Hello," he says. I imagine him in the kitchen of his home,
a small Cape in central Connecticut.

"Teddy?" I ask. I can hear loud music in the background; it
sounds like Billy Joel's *River of Dreams.*

"Hi, Mom," he says. "You okay?"

"Yeah," I say. "D'you have a minute? Can you talk?"

"Sure, Mom."

"You sure?"

"Sure. Hold on," he says. "Let me turn the music down."
Billy Joel's lyrics get softer and softer. "What is it?" Teddy asks.
"You sound weird."

"I need to tell you something." I hear myself sigh. "After
you left, there was more. Monday morning, I got a call, a call
from the Cape Elizabeth Department of Public Works."

"So? What did they want?"

"Remember there were two men in a pickup truck waiting
for the family to leave, waiting to fill in the grave?"

"Sure," Teddy says. I remember wondering why it took two guys to fill in such a little hole."

"Turns out they didn't like the looks of the urn."

The two workmen had taken the urn back to the main office. I say to Teddy, "The clerk told me the ashes were in the wrong kind of container." She had implied that all the folks at the commissioner's office thought the urn was definitely *from away!*

"Oh, shit," Teddy says. "Oh, crap! So what was the container supposed to be?"

"Plastic. Or metal. Or wood covered with plastic."

"Plastic," Teddy says incredulously.

"Yeah, so I had to go pick up the urn."

"You had to go get it? Where is it now?"

"I've got it," I say. "It's been rolling around on the floor of my back seat for three days."

"You in the car?" he asks.

"Yeah. Hold on." The traffic ahead of me is slowing down, and it's not clear why.

I brake the car and hear the urn thump against the back of the driver's seat. Traffic resumes, and I make a right hand turn onto Fowler Road, the shortcut to the cemetery. "So, I've got your Grandma Iris in the back seat."

"Weird," Teddy says. "So what happened?"

"I had to call Lily. You can imagine."

"She must have been pissed."

"She was terribly angry." Lily had been furious but polite to me. "I'm sure she yelled at the funeral director. He called the Cape Elizabeth Commissioner of Public Works."

"The commissioner? Cape Elizabeth has a commissioner for cemeteries?"

"Well," I say egged on by Teddy's interest. "How about a commissioner for cemeteries, parks, recreational facilities, and trails?" I can feel myself edging close to hysteria. "It does seem like overkill. Did you hear that? I made a joke. Overkill."

"I heard it, Mom. Don't get carried away." I can hear him running water and swallowing.

"Anyway, it took a lot of calls back and forth. The commissioner was concerned the urn was glass or ceramic. That wasn't good."

"So? Did it get straightened out?"

"Finally," I say. I turn at the grange hall, hear the urn rolling behind me. I can see the steeple of the white chapel ahead of me. "Teddy, that's why I'm calling. I just got an all clear from the clerk. She says the urn is metal. I can take your Grandmother Iris back to the cemetery."

"So you can bury her after all?"

"Yeah, I can."

I should be feeling more relieved than I do. But I've gotten used to Iris being in the car; I've gotten used to being careful around every corner, remembering her presence, even apologizing to her when I take a corner too fast. "It's going to sound strange to you," I say, "but I'm going to miss her."

"Mom," Teddy asks. "You okay?"

"I'm going to miss her," I say.

"Jesus," Teddy says, "I wish I was there. You sound a little strained. Maybe this has been too much for you."

"Oh, Teddy. I'm doing okay." I do feel a little teary. "It's just odd. I didn't like your grandmother. But I loved her."

"Mom, you okay? Maybe you should have a cup of herbal tea when you get home."

"I wish I had an Ativan." I check the traffic behind me and turn into the empty cemetery. My Camry's tires crunch on the gravel as I turn down the lane to Iris's open grave.

"I'm in the cemetery," I say to Teddy. "Just a second." I pull the car to a gentle stop. "Would you mind holding on for a couple of seconds? I'm going to put the urn in the ground."

I insert a Pavarotti CD into my car's music player; a Puccini aria begins. I turn it up.

"What?" Teddy asks. "What's with the music? You playin' opera for Grandma?"

"I am. I thought she might like a little Pavarotti as a send-off." I get out of my Camry, open the back door and lift the cloisonné urn with its beautiful swirls of red and gold. I speak loudly through the open window of the front door. "I'm going now, Teddy." This should be quick. "I'll be right back."

I carry the urn carefully. When I get to the square of green plastic grass, I kneel on it, bend over, and lower the urn into the small grave. "Iris, if this is you, I hope you'll be at peace. Miriam, if these are your ashes, I hope you think this is a beautiful place."

When I return to the car, settle into the front seat, and turn off the music, I ask, "Teddy, you there?"

"Yes. You finished?"

"I am," I say. "The urn is returned."

"So what was the urn made of?" Teddy asked.

"Metal with glass decoration."

"Mom, anything else you need me for?"

"No, you've been wonderful. You're such a good son. You were a good grandson, too." I pause. "Would you say a prayer for Iris?"

"You know I don't pray much, Mom."

How about something short and simple?"

"What about Miriam? Shouldn't she get a prayer?" I can hear him laughing. He's teasing me.

"Be serious for a minute, Teddy."

"The hospital keeps me pretty busy," he says. Teddy is working as a physician's assistant at a children's hospital in their ER. The irony isn't lost on me; he's saving lives just as his life was saved. I feel apologetic for asking him to do me a favor until he says, "Mom, email me a short prayer for Grandma. I'll say it."

"Thank you," I say. "I love you, Teddy."

"Love you, too, Mom."

THE FOLLOWING DAY, I email an abbreviated prayer to Teddy:

"We see them now with the eye of memory,
Their faults forgiven, their virtues grown larger,
So does goodness live and weakness fade from sight."

From *Gates of Prayer, The New Union Prayer Book*,
Central Conference of American Rabbis, New York, 1975,
p. 550.

And so, we remember Iris. And Miriam.

t h i r t e e n

THE PHOTOGRAPH

After my father dies in 1995, a year after Geoff's death, I increase the frequency of my visits to Montana. Three or four times a year, I travel cross-country to my hometown to spend a week with my mother. Those weeks can seem long. My mother is demanding—she has a long list of tasks for me on every trip home. But I do look forward to her family stories. She loves to talk about her father, a tall Scotsman with a red beard. And she keeps my father alive for both of us by telling me stories about him. One of the high points of my visits is when I read aloud a certain letter from their courtship days at the University of Montana; in it, my father calls a rival suiter a chipmunk. She and I laugh with abandon.

Years ago, at age seventy, my mother suddenly lost her frontal vision to macular degeneration. Her adaptation was amazing, especially her ability to maintain social contacts. She is excellent at communicating what she needs. I'm used to her ordering me around and have given up trying to resist. She often reminds me, "When you sit across from me, I can't see your face." Her vision, she explains, is blocked by what she describes as a continent-like shape; in her eighties, she still has peripheral vision, but it is diminishing. She has taught me to sit next to her.

When I am not in Billings, nurse's aides come in twice a day to assist her with showering and dressing, and to prepare meals for her. Despite her age, she is clear-minded and able to listen to current bestsellers and classics on tape, to work on family genealogy with a Mormon woman, and to keep track of her finances.

"Come and sit here," my mother pats her brightly colored bedspread. I comply. If I am quiet, my mother may share a story I have never heard before.

"When your dad was away in the Pacific," she says, "I would look at a photograph of him that I loved. He was in a Donegal tweed suit that I had helped him pick out. It had a matching vest. He looked so handsome, athletic, and happy." She reaches across and pats one of my hands. I think she is near tears, but she continues. She says, "When I looked at that photograph, I could see the man I fell in love with at the University of Montana."

I hold her hand as she remembers both the photograph and the man. I let the silence linger.

"The photo," my mother says, "was from before the war, before Pearl Harbor. Your dad and I had been married almost ten years. He was teaching history at the high school in Carson City, Nevada. I had other photos, but the one of your dad in the tweed suit was my favorite."

I am familiar with some photos of my father, ones taken of him as a newly commissioned naval officer, and later photos of my father in his uniform looking serious, even somber. But I have never heard about this photo, her favorite.

"After Pearl Harbor, your father enlisted. He went to Tower Hall in Chicago for officer training." So far, this information is familiar. I have been told that the famous pianist, Eddy Duchin and JFK were at Tower Hall at the same time as my father.

"After that," my mother says, "I moved to be wherever your father was. First to Miami, then to New York. I had a good job there. You know about that." I do. She worked in the translation department of an organization that later evolved into the United Nations. While she was in New York, she kept a scrapbook of playbills and invitations to teas and bridge games for officers' wives.

"Then," my mother says, "I lived in Newport, Rhode Island. Your father would be in and out of port." I know that once my mother became pregnant, my father sent her to live with her sister in Montana. He believed she would get more personal medical care somewhere other than a military hospital.

"After you were born," my mother says, "your dad was sent to amphibious training in California. We had a little apartment in Coronado. He would be gone long days, but come home every night."

"I remember that," I say. I've heard about Coronado before. And been there.

"But when your father went away to the Pacific, I never knew where he was. He couldn't tell me. I read *Time* and *Life* magazines, looked at the photos of Iwo Jima and Okinawa. I worried about where he might be. I cried."

I'm silent because I don't want to interrupt this story, one I've never heard before.

My mother says, "I would go into our closet and bury my face in your father's tweed jacket. It smelled like pipe smoke and for a few seconds, I was with your dad."

My mother sighs, and I put my arm around her. "Oh, Mom," I say.

"Before your dad was in the Navy," she says, "before he went to war, he was light-hearted. He was part Irish you know," she says. "Your Grandmother Mary loved to laugh and to joke. And so did your dad."

I remember my Grandma Mary with a glass of bourbon laughing with my Great Uncle Hal. Even as a child, I sensed he was telling her off-color jokes.

"Nance," my mother says, "I waited and waited for the war to end. Your dad was gone for so long. When he was in Tokyo Bay for the surrender of the Japanese, we both thought he would be coming right home. Other husbands came home. But not your dad."

I remember a small black and white photo of my dad aboard his ship, the USS Rutland, in Tokyo Bay.

"Your dad finally came home. Months later. I had been raising you alone. I didn't know much about his life in the Navy. And he never talked about it."

"I know," I say. My father never spoke of his experiences in WWII.

"I guess I didn't know much about what he went through," my mother says.

"Probably not," I say. "But, Mom, what about the photograph of Dad, the one you liked so much. Where is it?"

"Oh," she says. "One day, I was so angry. I thought that the Navy had taken away the man I loved." She turns her face to me. "You see the man who came home wasn't my John, wasn't the man I had fallen in love with."

I murmur. I'm straining to understand. "So, what happened to the photo?" I ask.

"Nance, I was so angry. I just tore the photograph up into little pieces."

"You tore it up?" I ask.

"Yes," she says. "I liked it the best, and I tore it up."

f o u r t e e n

LAST WORDS

Thank you for coming," I say to Simon as we ride the elevator up to my mother's condo on the seventh floor of a high rise with its beautiful view of the Beartooth Mountains. "You sounded like you needed some company on this trip west," Simon says. "How often have you been coming?" "Every three or four months." I sigh. "Then also for emergencies. Like now." My older son and I are in my hometown in the spring of 2004 because my ninety-two year old mother fell, suffered a head injury, and was taken by ambulance to the local hospital.

As soon as Simon opens the front door of my mother's home, we can see evidence that a rescue team has been here. The colonial-style settee from the entryway has been dragged into the dining area. And hand-embroidered cushions and mail have been spilled onto the thick wool carpeting. Simon and I roll our suitcases through the disarray and switch on the lights. Otherwise, the condo seems to look as it usually does. In the living room, every glass tabletop is adorned with family photos and pottery; my mother's tape player and a stack of books-on-tape sit on the sofa.

"Mom, come look at this," Simon calls from my mother's bedroom.

"Oh, God!" I say discovering a head-sized blood stain on the pale green carpeting near the foot of her bed. I know my mother fell, suffered a head wound, but I am unprepared for the extent of the blood.

"Jesus," Simon says. "That was one hell of a fall." He looks shaken.

I close the bedroom door. Simon heads for the kitchen and a beer.

Suddenly, I'm exhausted. "It's almost midnight in our bodies," I say. I began the day in Portland, Maine, traveled to Boston by bus, met Simon at Logan, flew to O'Hare, then Denver, then Billings. I pour myself a glass of generic white wine. "I'm going to bed."

The next morning, Simon and I are up early; we shower and dress and afterward, with only orange juice and English muffins for breakfast, we drive to the hospital. I want to be sure to be in time for doctors' rounds. When we arrive at my mother's room, her doctor introduces himself. I remind him of her impaired vision and hearing, encourage him to stand close and to speak up.

"Hello, Mrs. Bills," he calls out to my mother. "I don't suppose you remember me. I was one of your English students at West High School.

My mother is polite but lukewarm in response. I doubt she remembers him, one of so many students. He theorizes that low blood pressure was likely the cause of her fall; he recommends an adjustment of medication, and my mother agrees. He says, "As soon as your vital signs improve, you can be discharged."

"Mrs. Bills," he chuckles as he is leaving, "you were a tough teacher, quite a stickler about grammar." He doesn't have to tell me. I'll never forget that she sent my letters from Colorado College back to me with red-penciled corrections.

After the doctor is gone, my mother confirms my suspicions. "I have no idea who that young man is," she says.

Over pancakes and bacon at the hospital cafeteria, Simon agrees with me that his grandmother still seems strong and her thinking appears clear in spite of her fall. We would both like her to sell her condo and move to an assisted living facility here; long ago, she dismissed the idea of moving east and interacting with easterners!

Since my father's death, I've heard her reasons for not wanting to move, most of them related to her near-blindness. She values the control she has over her surroundings; she knows where everything is in her condo. If she moves to a facility, a staff member or resident might drop something in her path; she might trip over it and fall. Also the nurse's aides who come twice a day are answerable to her; after all, she's the one who pays them. Those are her rational arguments. A more mysterious one is her belief that my father's spirit visits her at night and that if she moves, he wouldn't be able to find her. I don't know how to respond to that. What can I say?

I respect my mother's arguments, her personal take on safety and danger, but now that she has taken a bad fall, maybe she will feel differently. I hope so.

By the time Simon and I finish our breakfast, I'm beginning to wonder if it was necessary for us to race across more than a half dozen states to be at my mother's bedside. "I'm sorry I dragged you out here," I say.

"It's okay, Mom. I know these visits are hard on you," Simon says smiling indulgently. "At least this time, you're not alone."

Simon and I take turns sitting with my mother. She sleeps much of the day. When she wakens, she checks on what I have been reading, always encouraging me to reread classics especially Jane Austen. I contact my mother's cleaning lady who is already at the condo working on the blood stain on the bedroom rug.

"It won't come out," Juanita says. "It's going to require professional cleaning."

Midafternoon, I return to my mother's room to discover Simon and his grandmother discussing a Theodore Roosevelt biography. Although I have read it too, I leave the conversation to the two of them. Later, Simon and I sit with my mother while she has her dinner tray. Afterward, when the nurse comes in, my mother says, "Go along, you two. Get some supper." We will see her in the morning.

As we walk out to the parking lot, Simon says, "How about The Cattlemen's Grill?"

"Yes," I say opening the passenger door. What a good idea. I'm immediately dreaming of a rare filet mignon. Nothing like Montana beef.

THE NEXT MORNING, we arrive at the hospital in time for doctors' rounds again. A nurse stops us in front of my mother's room. "She's not here. She fell in the bathroom this morning. A broken arm."

"Oh," I moan. "Poor mother."

"Where is she?" Simon asks.

"First, she was taken to X-ray. The arm requires surgery. So now she's in pre-op." The nurse begins to give us instructions.

"I know where that is," I tell Simon. We race to the surgical wing and arrive in time to see my tiny mother in a blue-flowered hospital gown bundled in white blankets on a gurney.

"Mom," I say taking her good hand. "I'm so sorry. Are you in pain?"

"No, dear. I'll be fine. Try not to worry."

I'm not sure if my mother realizes she's a poor risk for anesthesia. What if she dies? What if I'm seeing her for the last time? "I love you, mother," I say.

"Let me talk to Simon," she asks beckoning for him.

"Of course," I say. Perhaps my mother wants to share some last wise words with her elder grandson. Or perhaps she wishes to tell him how much she loves him. I feel a wave of warmth sweep over me. I watch as Simon bends over the gurney and strains to hear his grandmother. He is sensitive; I am proud of him. When he raises his head, he looks puzzled rather than pleased. Without a moment's delay, masked attendants roll my mother through double doors into surgery.

"What did she say?" I ask Simon.

He shakes his head and points toward the elevator. "Let's go to the cafeteria."

We sit across from each other at an orange Formica table. Simon has a cup of tea; me, too. Each of us has a cardboard box of corn flakes with small carton of milk. We pick up our plastic spoons. "What in the world did she say?" I ask.

"Grandma said that there's been something she's wanted to tell me for a long time."

I can feel my face frown, my whole body frown.

"What?"

"She wants me to know that sometimes I misuse a gerund."

"You misuse a gerund?"

"Yes, Mom. That's what she said."

f i f t e e n

IN THE SHOWER

A year later, my mother is ninety-three, and I'm back in Montana. She was hospitalized briefly for dehydration. She has been discharged in my care.

"PLEASE, MOM," I say, "we need to stop and get you out of here." I glance at the tile walls of her master bath's shower.

"No," my mother protests, "There's still shampoo in my hair. I want my hair washed. Just steady me. That's what Donna does." Donna is her nurse's aide, the aide she cancelled because I was coming.

"Mom, it's just you and me." She staggers a little. Her brief burst of strength is fading.

"Just steady me."

"Okay." I place my arms firmly around her middle and brace myself. "Just put your head under the water once, and then, that's it. You're still weak. You just got out of the hospital." My mother leans forward; I can feel rather than see the showerhead spray the top of her head. Warm water splashes my face and neck. Now the front and sleeves of my aqua turtleneck are soaked. But at least as I look down, the water at the bottom of the shower has turned from soapy to clear.

"Okay, shampoo's out." But when I look at my mother's face, I know we have waited too long. Her lips are blue and quivering; her whole body is trembling. She isn't saying a word. My mother is usually articulate and opinionated. She gave her high school English students poor grades if they chewed gum. During my quarterly visits from Maine, she has routinely criticized my clothing choices saying, "Don't wear jeans, and no black; black isn't a color at all!" She has chided me, "You sound just like a social worker." And I was not supposed to be a social worker. I wasn't the English professor she had dreamed of. But now she is frightened; now she is silent.

You can be so stupid, I say to myself. *This is the worst thing you've ever done. Your mother is going to die in your arms. How will you explain to anyone that she's dead because you thought you could give her a shower and shampoo her hair? That's why there are nurse's aides!*

My fears well up. *How will you explain to the ambulance team that she's not only dead but also naked and wet?* I have been stupid before—mostly romantic stuff, adolescent crushes and young adult loves that just wouldn't let go, but now my little sparrow of a mother is chilled to her tiny core. If I don't get her circulation churned up, she is going to have a heart attack or a stroke.

You're the most dangerous kind of person, I tell myself. *Well-intentioned.* A prayer spills out of me, *Oh God, have mercy on me. Oh God, forgive me. Don't let my mother die on my watch. Find some other way to punish me.* Soaking wet, scared to death, I have the impulse to genuflect.

"Hold on," I say. "Let's get you out of here." My mother's high-rise condo, Rocky Mountain Heights, usually seems luxurious, but now, all the features of the bathroom including the glass shower door, even the four-inch threshold, are obstacles to moving her into her bedroom. She clings to me with her age-spotted hands, but her bony, narrow feet aren't providing support. "Try to stand," I say with gravity, and she responds. I hit the glass shower door with my left elbow. It swings open. "Shit," I whisper. I have banged the funny bone. "Here we go."

"No."

"Mom, we've got to get you out of here." I sound surprisingly severe.

"Oh. Ohhh," the words come out of her mouth like those out of a woman who can't fight a rogue wave or an undertow. I am the unexpected wave. She is the mother and used to being a force to be reckoned with. But now, I am the authority. If she doesn't look better within a few minutes all truly bundled up in bed, I will call 9-1-1. I shift her weight to my right shoulder and hip.

"Now," I say. She resists initially, but then I can feel her helping, doing her feeble best. My right side is used to taking the burden of lifting and carrying since my left shoulder is a wreck. The joint was cracked and the rotator cuff massively torn in a horseback-riding accident, another example of my stupidity. *Why did I ever think I could ride a horse?* But in my defense, I did stay on my mare through four bucks, just not through the fifth one.

As we make our awkward way across the carpeted bathroom, I grab a big handful of towels out of the linen closet. A whole pile falls creating a pink and green trail, but I manage to drape one towel around my mother's wet, gray head and another around her shoulders, which aren't much more than skin-covered bones. I wind a big bath towel around her middle while we take the last steps to her bed.

I sweep the covers back.

"What?" she asks.

"Get in, and I'll cover you up."

She nods and lies down. I take a few seconds to dry her wet hair and wind a fresh dry towel around her head. Then I cover her from head to foot with dry towels and pull up the sheet, blanket, and bedspread, pretty with yellow flowers. I start to walk away from her. "Don't go," she says. "Got to if I'm going to warm you up." I stride to the doorway of her bedroom to the thermostat. I click it up to seventy-five degrees and close the door.

Upon my return to her bedside, I study her face. She is hyperventilating. "No, Mom," I say. "Please don't do that." She looks startled. "Look at me. Breathe with me." I know this drill. I've done it multiple times with anxious patients, with patients suffering panic attacks. "Breathe in through your nose," I whisper. "Then let it out slowly through your mouth. Slowly. Slowly." We breathe together. "Hmm, good," I encourage her. My breath becomes hers, and hers, mine. We practice breathing together.

"MOM," I SAY solemnly, "I'm going to take out one arm or leg at a time and dry it thoroughly. I'll keep all the rest of you covered. Then if you're still okay . . ." This seems like a big *if*. "Then, we'll tackle putting your clothes on. Do you understand?"

She signs on and cooperates as I not only dry her limbs but also chafe them to improve her blood flow. The air in the room is warming up. I am feeling more hopeful, but I am still aware that in an instant, something can go wrong. That's the mantra of my life: *Life looks good right now, but things can go to hell any minute.* Lightning is rare, but it does strike. I know.

I hand my mother a small, pink guest towel with eyelet trim to dry her pubic area while I search for comfortable clothes, pants with an elastic waist, a top with a zipper front. I grab a faded blue velour pantsuit. "Let's just start with socks and see how you do."

She is relieved to be getting dressed. She insists on underpants and a bra, "the beige ones with lace." I think we could have done without a bra, but getting dressed goes well. I examine her face. It isn't just my wishful thinking. Her color looks better, and she has stopped trembling. I tuck her under the covers. "I'll bring you some tea and toast." She looks worried, but she nods. I speed out to the kitchen and make the fastest tea and toast of my life. But not without an accompanying silent prayer, *Thank you, God, whoever you are—male, female, inside or outside of me. Thank you.* Mom drinks the tea and eats the toast. She sends me to the kitchen to get sugar for her tea. It's a good sign; she is ordering me around.

Then she says, "You need to do my hair."

"Okay," I say searching for a hair dryer and brush. "I'll do the best I can, but it won't look the way you're used to." Later, I show her the rather sad results in a mirror.

"It's okay," she says, "but you're not much of a beautician." That is about as close as my mother comes to humor. She smiles. "You should know something about yourself, Nance."

"What?" I hate to imagine what.

"Dear, I was frightened. You were scared, too. I could tell." She takes a sip of her tea and says, "I haven't always been a good mother."

"Oh, Mom. I don't think now is the time."

"Let me finish. When we were in the shower, I learned something, something I should have known before. You should know you're a good person."

I just let that sink in. I had been waiting for these words all my adult life.

"I should sleep now," she says.

I'm no nurse, but she seems pretty normal. I pause at the doorway. I say, "Mom, call if you need me."

"I'm okay," she says, "If I were going to die, I think I'd be dead by now."

sixteen

MAKING AN EXIT

On a different visit home, it's three in the morning when my alarm clock wakens me. Beep, beep. Beep, beep! The annoying noise is unrelenting. *Get up. Get up. Say goodbye to your mother. Catch your plane.* The guest room was warm when I turned the thermostat down at midnight, but now it is chilly. I watched a rerun of *Yellowstone in Winter* until Montana PBS went off the air. Now I wish I had gotten more sleep.

I pull the drapes back and look out on the well-lit entrance of The Rockies, a senior care facility in my childhood home. The roads and sidewalks are covered with at least the eight inches of the snow forecast on the local news last night. Wet snowflakes from the last spring storm of 2007 pummel the windows.

My selection of clothing for the plane trip home is in a neat pile on the cheery bedspread. I make a couple of clothing corrections—a substitution of wool socks for cotton, the addition of gloves and a muffler. I reposition my week's worth of clothes in my rolling suitcase. I wore almost everything I packed although it's harder than one might think to anticipate weather differences between Maine and Montana.

Some daughters might have showered the previous night, but I know from many prior visits that I need a shock of water to wake me. I need to be alert for my exit and trip home. After I drop my pajamas on the cold tiles of the bathroom floor, I duck into the handicap-accessible shower. I think how it's strange to be a resident in a "facility" before one's time. But staying in a guest room has been convenient because The Rockies is miles outside Billings in the middle of the tumbleweed-strewn prairie of central Montana. If I'd stayed at a friend's or at a hotel, much of my week-long visit to my mother would have been squandered driving back and forth.

Showered, shampooed, and dressed in jeans, a wool cardigan, and a light parka, I drag my suitcase into the hallway and take the elevator to the first floor. I drop my room key off at the main entryway desk. No staff. It's disturbingly quiet. I hurry past the doors to the chapel; I say goodbye to walls of western art—herds of cattle behind miles of barbed-wire fencing and forests with snarling wolves and toothy grizzly bears. I cut across the formal dining room with its tables laid out for breakfast—white tablecloths, vases of daisies. Then I begin the long circuitous journey from Independent Living to Assisted Living, from the west wing to the east.

I elbow my way through an "Employees Only" door and start the Nancy Drew portion of my shortcut, a back hallway past the kitchen with its confusion of odors and the staff break-room with its glowing wall of vending machines. I re-enter the public area stepping from scarred linoleum onto sculpted carpeting. As I roll my suitcase past assisted living doorways, I wonder what the various floral wreaths say about the sleeping occupants within.

It takes all my shortcuts to arrive at my mother's door by 4:00 a.m. Inside her apartment, I tiptoe through the small living room to the doorway of her bedroom. My mother has lost so much weight that her body barely creates a silhouette under her floral coverlet. I pause and breathe. I prepare for a probable last goodbye.

"Mother," I say patting her shoulder. "It's Nancy."

"Oh, Nance," she says immediately. "You came. You didn't have to. Is it already time?"

"Yes, Mom." I study the room as if I am a camera; the urn with my father's ashes rests on my mother's bedside table. My father always honored.

My mother weakly raises her head. "It's meant so much to have you here. We had a pretty good time. Didn't we?" I nod. "And I enjoyed the trip by the old house." I'm glad she was strong enough to go for a brief ride.

"What time is it?" she asks.

"A little after four," I say. I'll need all the time I've planned to drive to the airport, drop off the rental, and process through security. I half expect my flight to be cancelled. But I need to go. *Don't I?*

In three days, I have surgery scheduled at home. My hands fly up to my neck, my troublesome thyroid, the offending body part with the possible tumor.

"You need to go. Don't you?"

"Yes, Mom." I take in a great breath. "I love you," I say.

"You're a good girl." We are both silent. "You go along. I'll fall right back to sleep," she says. "Go. Go along."

I kiss her forehead; it feels talcum-dry to my lips. Her blind eyes close, and her faint breathing lengthens.

"Goodbye, Mom."

The trip back to the main entrance of The Rockies is a blur. I rummage through my shoulder purse to find my plane tickets and the keys to my rental car. My rollaway suitcase catches first on ridges in the carpeting and then in ditches in the tile flooring. *You're doing okay*, I say to myself as I check my watch. *Just keep moving.*

The double doors at the main entrance shock me; they refuse to open; I let my suitcase collapse at my feet. I stamp on the ribbed rubber floor in an attempt to trigger the automatic door mechanism. No response. I search the surrounding walls for a button, a sensor. Nothing. I even kick the doors. *Time is ticking away,* I think. *Try another entrance.*

I run down a hallway clumsily dragging my rollaway. I do find an alternate exit. And yes, it opens. I step through. Snowflakes cover my glasses. I can't see, but I am outside. I take a large gulp of cold air.

My suitcase is awkward on the un-shoveled walkways and a strain in the slushy parking lot. But somehow, I hoist it onto the back seat. I press my already tired body behind the steering wheel and fasten my seat belt. When I shift the engine into reverse, the light compact car slides backward and down a slight incline. Directly ahead is a The Rockies sign; the American flag and Montana state flag are whipping in the wind. I apply the gas gingerly and attempt to go forward. But the car does a little buck. Immediately, I press the accelerator firmly down, but the car resists and bucks again crazily lurching from side to side. I stop the car, turn off the engine. I let out the great breath I've been holding in.

You'll never make it to the airport, I think. *The plane will leave without you. You've got to do something.*

And I do. I realize in a split second that I have not released the brake. The emergency brake has caused the problem. As soon as I release the brake, the tires are able to make traction despite the snow and slight grade. Within moments, I am stopping at the EXIT sign; turning right, I am headed for Billings International Airport.

I will avoid Stagecoach Trail with its dangerous switchbacks, but even Airport Hill Road will be daunting, slippery. If only the rental car will trudge faithfully up the snowy road to the airport built so precariously on a high sandstone bluff. If only the snow stops and the visibility clears. If only, so many ifs.

If only I am allowed a graceful exit.

s e v e n t e e n

THE PATRIOTS'
DAY STORM

When the ringing of my cell phone wakens me, I know it must be the nurse from Rocky Mountain Hospice calling. "It's mother's nurse," I whisper to David, my friend and lover of six years; he is lying next to me in the dark. "Yes, Sharon," I say into my phone. "Thank you for calling." She apologizes that it's late or early. I'm not sure which.

"How is my mother?" I ask, and Sharon shares her report. "Is she in any pain?" I ask. "No?" The details flow over me, and I repeat part of what I am hearing so David will know. ". . . so running a high fever and her heartbeat is fainter." I sigh. "Thank you," I say. "Thank you for your kindness."

"Well," David asks, "What did she say?"

"She thinks my mother is going to die today."

"How can she tell?" he asks. This is typical David, ever the skeptic.

"She's a hospice nurse. She's seen a lot of death."

He reaches out and tries the bedside lamp. "Power's out."

"I'm not surprised," I say, "Central Maine Power is going to be busy." We are both silent. "Tell me what day it is," I ask.

"It's April the sixteenth," he says. "It's Patriots' Day in Massachusetts. I bet they'll have to cancel the Boston Marathon because of the storm."

"Mother would have been ninety-five if she'd lived till her birthday in June."

"She hasn't died yet," he says. "You just saw her. Did it seem like she was dying?"

"I worried that I might not see her again," I say. "And she was . . . fragile." I silently repeat the dates of my mother's birth and anticipated death—*June 16, 1912 to April 16, 2007. Patriots' Day, 2007. I'll remember this,* I tell myself, *like I remember other dates. Like July 24, 1994.*

By the time I do a lot of reminiscing, David is asleep. *I better get out of bed,* I think. *Maybe the nurse will call back, and I want to be ready.* As I swing out of bed into the pitch dark, somehow my feet find my slippers; as I reach out into the chilly air, my hands find the footboard to guide me through the sightless space. At the doorway of the bedroom, I run my hands over the familiar walls. I try the hall and bathroom lights. No response.

IT IS 9:00 a.m. I sit on the couch in the dimly lit living room still in my pajamas, the cornflower blue ones with old-fashioned full-blown roses. I reach down and pat the blue fleece of my winter robe and retie its belt. The heat from the gas fireplace burns my cheeks yet the living room is cold and drafty. I run the cool back of my right hand across my face. Soon the first floor will warm up. Soon the power will be back on. Soon the storm will be over.

Outdoors, the threatening wind drives sheet after sheet of rain onto the east-facing windows; the half-shuttered windows usually offer a view of the Portland seaway, but not now. At intervals when the rain reaches crescendos, a thin layer of water seeps between the window moldings and bleeds down the panes.

I love the giant maple tree outside for its ability to soothe me, but now its newly leafed- out branches are thrust in helpless arcs. *Oh, please don't fall down,* I say to the tree. *I love you. Don't die. Let it be some other tree.* But I catch myself; I can't pray for that.

Sometime later, I hear David's footsteps on the stairs.

"Power's still out," I say, "but there's orange juice and cereal."

From the kitchen, he calls out, "If you open the refrigerator, do it quickly so the food won't spoil."

"I know," I say. I am a veteran of storms and power outages in rural New Hampshire and Maine.

"How long have you been up?"

"Since the nurse's phone call."

"When was that?" he asks.

"About seven, I think."

"I'm sorry."

"I know."

"Do you think the nurse can really tell?" he asks.

"Yes," I say. "Remember she's a hospice nurse. A nurse begins to recognize the signs—changes in breathing, changes in the color of the skin, even the tilt of the chin."

"How do you feel?" he asks.

"Sad."

"No," he says pointing to his own neck. "I mean, your neck, the incision?"

"Oh, it hurts," I say touching the semi-circle of bandages that cover the three incisions. "It's tender. But, of course, I'm awfully relieved not to have thyroid cancer."

David nods and looks at the bleary world outside the windows. "I want to go look at Willard Beach," he says. "I want to check on how high the ocean is, to see if the beach is covered. Do you want to come?"

"I think I should stay by the phone."

"It may take hours," he says, but then he adds, "but I understand."

He comes into the living room and sits on the couch beside me. He holds his slicker loosely in his arms and stares into the orange and yellow flames of the fire.

"What time is it?" I ask him.

"Almost ten-thirty."

"Could you wait just a little?"

"Sure."

We sit quietly for nearly half an hour.

And then the phone rings.

e i g h t e e n

BURIAL AT SEA

Still in my pajamas and robe, I'm sitting on my sofa staring at the flames of my gas fireplace. David has returned from checking the damage to the Willard Beach neighborhood by today's storm—tree limbs down, the beach covered with debris. It's midday when my cell phone rings.

"Nancy Bills?" an unfamiliar male voice asks.

"Yes, this is Nancy."

"This is Walter Wilson of the Evergreen Funeral Home in Billings returning your call. I understand your mother, Maggie Bills, has passed."

"Yes," I say.

"May I express the condolences of myself and my staff to you and your family?"

"Thank you," I say. "Have you heard from the nursing home?"

"Yes," he says. "I was just leaving to remove the body." He stops himself. "I'm just going to transport your mother to our funeral home."

We both pause. I try to block out the inevitable image.

"Do you have a minute?" Walter asks. "I want to review your instructions."

"Yes, of course."

"You want your mother's remains to be cremated and to have a memorial service at the Presbyterian Church on Rimrock Road."

"Yes," I say. "And you should have a copy of the obituary."

"Yeah, found it," he says. "Can I fax it to the *Gazette?*"

"Yes, please." He means *The Billings Gazette.* "You'll need to insert today's date."

"Yeah, I already did," he says. "April 16, 2007. She lived a long life. Just two months shy of ninety-five."

"Yes," I say.

"Can you hold for a minute or two?" he asks.

"Sure." The power is still out in my condo—no lights, but I have heat from the gas fireplace and a mug of hot tea. I stand and look down at the pattern of my living room rug—flowers, leaves at my feet.

My mother is dead, and I wasn't with her. I bend over a persistent puddle in front of the sliding glass door and mop at the rain water with a dish towel. Outdoors, the hurricane-level winds have slowed, but the sky is still gray and threatening. News announcers on my emergency radio are calling the frightening winds and torrential rain the Patriots' Day Storm.

Holding the phone to my chest, I mouth to my partner, David, "I should go."

He shakes his head. "No, you shouldn't," he says. He points to my neck. "You just had surgery. You can't go anywhere. Besides Boston, Logan Airport, is closed."

I reach up and feel the bandages, the Steri-strips, that cover my incision, really three incisions around my neck.

DR. GILLIAN, MY surgeon, explained to me, "Your neck is curved so I can't make one incision; I'll have to make three." I must have looked frightened. He continued, "Don't worry.

When the stitches heal, you'll barely be able to see them." Later, after my surgery, he reported, "Your thyroid's been removed. Good news. No cancer."

I HEAR THE phone receiver in Montana being picked up. Walter asks, "Nancy?"

"Yes."

"I found the obituary. It's long. It'll be expensive."

"I know."

Mother and I wrote her obituary as though it were a master's thesis—research, rough drafts, rewrites, editing, and more editing. On one visit home, I suggested we cut some of the material. I said, "This is more about Dad than about you, Mom."

"I don't want a word changed," she said.

"Mom, this bit about me shouldn't be in here. People don't need to know that I was in Brownies and that you were my Brownie leader."

"I like the parts about you."

"But they shouldn't be in your obituary. They could go in a family narrative. What if I take the obituary home to Maine and do some editing? I'll be sure to save the parts about Dad." I knew how proud my mother was to be the widow of a naval officer.

"I want you to include your father's World War II service, his bronze star. And about him being in Tokyo Bay for the surrender of the Japanese."

"I know, Mom."

"NANCY? ARE YOU there?" Walter asks me as though he knows my mind has been wandering.

"Yes?"

"Your mother wanted her ashes mingled with your father's? Right?" I make a small assenting noise. "Where are your father's ashes?"

"They're on mother's bedside table in a walnut urn. Can you pick it up when you transport my mother?"

"Yeah, sure I can. And don't worry about the details. I understand you just had surgery."

How does he know? Oh, I suppose I told him. Now, all of Billings knows.

"We'll take care of things here," Walter says. "You get some rest."

SEVERAL YEARS BEFORE my mother died, she gave me specific directions. "I want your dad's and my ashes mingled and then scattered. You can drive up to the airport and scatter some off the Rimrocks. Then, you can go to the Yellowstone Country Club. Ask the golf 'pro', Paul, to borrow a golf cart. Scatter some along the fairways and on the greens; your father's favorites were number five and number fourteen. And then, I want you to go to Coronado in California. Remember our winter vacations to Coronado? Ask Wilbur Seagle to get his sailboat out. You can scatter the rest in San Diego Bay."

In the last months before her death, my mother said to me, "You don't have to do all that. What was I thinking? So much trouble for you." I tried not to show my relief. She continued with her new instructions, "Just bury us in the plot at Lewis and Clark Cemetery next to your aunt and uncle. That'll be easy."

So no scattering of ashes from a sailboat, no burial at sea. Actually, I feel at sea. I think I probably will for a long, long while.

n i n e t e e n

AN ODE TO TAPIOCA

W hen my friend David was six, he was hit by a car. He was running across an intersection and then bam. When he first told me the story, I sensed that in those moments, his whole life was changed.

Now David describes the event with controlled emotion: he was being chased by school bullies; he was only a few blocks from his family's home on Perkins Road in Norwich, Connecticut. He was running; he was hit by a car. The astonished and frightened driver lifted his young, injured body, placed him in the back seat, and transported him to the local hospital. I suppose no driver would do that today. But those details somehow fit the story and the times, the neighborly 1940s.

David's parents were at work and didn't know for hours that he was in the hospital requiring surgery. And he endured surgery not just once, but twice. David's leg carries the legacy of his ordeal, a long jagged scar down the length of his left leg.

David is able to relate the story of his accident so that it sounds as though the accident and the month at William Backus Hospital happened to someone else, some boy he knew long ago before he grew a mustache and a beard, and his head became bald.

But that is not *the story.* The story is that while he was in the hospital, young David discovered a wonderful new food. For breakfast, he was served a delicacy that was salty, fatty, and scrumptious. He didn't know the name of the food. And he didn't taste the mysterious food again until he was at Dartmouth. In a college dining hall, he learned the name of the food. It was bacon.

He smiles now when he shares that from age six to eighteen, he never ate bacon. His family was Jewish and kept strictly kosher; any food from a pig was forbidden in his home. Now bacon is his favorite food.

I, TOO, AM fond of bacon. But the food that is remarkable in my life is tapioca. Isn't it intriguing how we humans can associate a food with pain, and conversely, with dependable comfort?

My first experience with tapioca, real tapioca, was in high school. My friend Karen invited several girlfriends to her home. Her mother, a home economics teacher, prepared something special for us. First, her mother began by separating the eggs and beating the multiple whites into froth. Later, I watched as her spatula dove and rose above her bowl in rhythmic motions folding a mixture of magic ingredients into the beaten egg whites. Karen's mother created a concoction of white pearls and golden foam.

My tongue and the roof of my mouth had never tasted, never touched anything so light and white and delicious. No words are round enough or sufficiently both delicate and bold to describe Mrs. Nelson's tapioca. It was stupendous.

IN AUGUST OF 1995, I journeyed from New Hampshire to Montana to spend the last weeks of my dad's life with him. He was a towering role model for dying well. His entire focus was on my mother and trying to prepare her for his death as if he were leaving on a long, long trip.

Mother was fiercely protective of my mild-mannered father. She was determined that he remain at home; she arranged for a hospital bed and hired nurse's aides to care for him. She supervised them carefully to assure that they were gentle, patient, and kind.

During those sad and painful days, I was impressed by how both my parents strained to spare the other. My dad didn't want to be a burden. My mother struggled to bear his imminent departure. Every night, she held onto my father's hands and whispered a prayer trying to assure him that they would never be separated.

In the midst of the poignancy of my father's dying, my mother and a nurse's aide from the local hospice had a terrible argument. The aide, who had a lot of experience with dying patients, brought homemade tapioca for my father; he was in great pain and had no appetite. But my mother's sense of control was threatened; she was furious.

"John," my mother declared, "has never liked tapioca. I don't think he's ever had tapioca." She paused and reviewed my father's food preferences during their sixty year-long marriage. "He likes red Jell-O with bananas, green Jell-O with canned pears. But never tapioca."

My dear father, weak as he was, asserted himself, "I do like tapioca. My mother used to make it for me when I was little."

"Oh, well," my mother relented. "If your mother made it for you, then I guess it's all right."

Not long after the thoughtful tapioca, my dad stopped eating altogether and died.

cᴐ℘ᴖ

IN JULY OF 1994, when my husband died both unexpectedly and violently, his sudden death caused a degree of shock that the death of my aging father did not. Only the death of a child posed a more profound loss.

And for three days—July the 24th, the 25th, and part of the 26th, I was frightened beyond description that I had not only lost my husband to lightning, but that I might also lose my younger son. During those three days of threat, I feared my son would not be able to breathe on his own. He lay on a hospital bed in the ICU, a tangle of tubes and wires connecting him to tenuous life, a harsh and noisy machine monitoring his every heartbeat.

Those days are a blur; I was numb with fear. I drifted from waiting room to ICU to waiting room. My memories—disconnected images and sensations, have no chronology. I do remember holding my injured son's hand and hugging my older son. And I remember the kindness of a nurse who pulled me out of my son's ICU room and sat me down in a chair at the nurses' station. I remember her thrusting a hot cardboard cup into my hand and telling me it was tea.

And I remember her directing me down a series of hallways to the cafeteria. The food choices were encased in plastic rectangles and triangles. There was only one food that I could imagine spooning into my mouth. And that was tapioca. And so during those terrible days, I drank tea and ate a few spoonfuls of tapioca.

Oh, mighty and dependable tapioca, what a godsend you are to those of us in need.

MY FRIEND DAVID loved me even though I'm not much of a cook. I bought boxes of pearl tapioca from the grocery store but never managed to actually prepare it. When he wasn't feeling well, I brought him store-bought chicken soup and Jell-O brand tapioca, and he was thankful. Even in its humblest form, tapioca is the most comforting of foods.

"Except," David would have said, "except for bacon."

t w e n t y

ATONEMENT

On September of 2009, David and I scoot along a wooden pew in Etz Chaim to make room for a couple of late arrivals, a man and his adolescent son, both of them hurrying to adjust yarmulkes on their heads and arrange prayer shawls around their shoulders. I notice that the yarmulkes are the white satin ones available at the rear of the synagogue, not the colorful and patterned ones that dot the backs of the heads of many men in the congregation.

David glances over at the father and son, murmurs a greeting that I imagine is the equivalent of "God be with you." Maybe something else, but not "Happy Yom Kippur." I don't understand Hebrew, but I understand this is a solemn holiday. The service begins with a mournful piece of music played by a thin but pretty woman. Cello music, David's favorite; he will be pleased.

Once a year, David comes to Etz Chaim, a three-story brick synagogue with arched stained-glass windows; built in 1921, the historical temple is hidden behind an iron fence and courtyard at the foot of Munjoy Hill in Portland, Maine. The inclusive, unconventional reform service is led by an elderly rabbi with stooped posture and wisps of white hair.

In the past, before I knew him, David fasted but not now;

given his age and his diabetes, he has decided that missing meals is unwise. And while he protests that he is a nonbeliever and attends only for the haunting Kol Nidre music, I am convinced that this vestige of his family's beliefs and rituals is meaningful for him. And it has become part of me, too. My imperfect understanding of the holy day stems from accompanying him for many years and his stories about his experiences growing up in an orthodox family.

I follow the order of service paging through the prayer book from right to left, standing and sitting, reading responsively in English, and listening respectfully to the Hebrew.

Despite my determination to concentrate on the prayers and readings, I am distracted. The essence of the day is to search one's life for regrets and to atone for them. And so, I retrieve two of mine.

IN 1994, I sat in another beautiful place of worship on an equally hard pew enduring a different ritual.

I regret that the memorial service for my late husband, Geoff, was not more in keeping with our family's history. Now as I look back, I regret asking Geoff's best friend to perform the service. What seems like an error in judgment now must have seemed like a perfect solution then. Geoff's best friend, Dr. Evan Royce, was a physician but also an Episcopalian priest.

I can see myself leave Teddy's hospital room on the med/surg floor at York Hospital and enter one of the small family waiting rooms. I stand beside a beige wall phone; I can even feel the cool plastic receiver in my hand and against my ear. I must have been tempted by the prospect of handing off the memorial service to Evan.

If I hadn't been in shock from having my husband and son

hit by lightning on a summer afternoon, I would have heard and responded immediately to Evan's hesitation. That's when I should have said, "Don't worry. I'll make some other arrangement." Then he could have added what he eventually did say, "Even though I'm a priest, I can't be the one to do the service. I'm too directly involved." But I was not quick enough to hear his ambivalence, and before I could respond, he had concluded, "The rector of the cathedral has agreed." And it was too late.

I remember Evan's words all these years later. "You're not the only one who has lost Geoff." And of course, he was right. Hundreds of colleagues, friends, and patients as well as family members would crowd St. Luke's, a traditional stone cathedral, a church I had never been in before.

I should not have had Geoff's service there, not have had an unfamiliar ritual performed by a stranger. I wish I could go back.

AFTER THE MEMORIAL service, I remember turning to Geoff's older sister, Sarah, and naively asking, "Isn't the church beautiful? Wasn't it lovely?" When she hesitated, frowned, why wasn't I prepared for her discomfort? I knew Geoff's family was Jewish.

However, in my defense, didn't everyone in the family have Christmas trees? When had any family member last been in a synagogue? Weren't they a secular family? Why, Geoff hadn't even had a bar mitzvah! The Passover Seders at my mother-in-law's were mostly about the food, the brisket, and potato pancakes; the readings from the Haggadah were always interrupted by complaints that they were too long. And hadn't Geoff's siblings all married Christians?

Still, now that I understand better how deeply ingrained Jewish identity is, I realize it was a mistake. Even though Geoff and I were married in a friend's garden in 1968, even though we were literally tied together by an Episcopal clergyman, I should have known better.

A service at the Unitarian Universalist church in Manchester would have been a more sensitive choice and equally as convenient for Geoff's mourners. When Geoff and I were newly married, the UU church with its focus on liberal social issues was a good compromise. When our sons were boys in Caribou, Maine, Geoff served on the church board; I made pies for bake sales and chicken stew for church dinners, the things women did in northern Maine. When we lived in Manchester, our sons attended UU Sunday school and summer camps. Geoff and I were comfortable with a church that was more like a philosophical debate.

And what about the little church in Deerfield? While fewer people would have made their way to the community church twenty miles east of Manchester, it would have been a fitting choice. After all, our family had gone to Christmas Eve services there for all the years we had lived in Deerfield; Geoff flipped hamburgers, and Teddy and I sold slices of pie at the church booth at the Deerfield Fairgrounds, the church's big annual fundraiser. And we attended services on the occasional Sunday.

No one in town would have held it against Teddy or me that we went trail riding most Sunday mornings or that I declared that spending time in the woods on horseback was our version of church; maybe our neighbors would have liked us all the better. More locals would have come to the modest church with its white steeple; more of the good folks who brought casseroles and brownies to the house after Geoff died would have crowded its plain interior.

So I wish I could go back and undo that. I wish I could say, "I'm sorry" to Sarah. And "I'm sorry" to Geoff's mother, Iris, who was grieving the loss of her youngest and didn't need to be enduring it in a church so undeniably Christian when a setting more like an Ethical Culture Society or reform temple would have suited me and my sons just as well. Wasn't it enough that for the first time, Iris was meeting my parents, the man and woman who had refused to attend a wedding twenty-six years previously because the groom's family was Jewish.

Perhaps Geoff would not have considered my decision to be an act of disloyalty, even a betrayal; I was almost sure that he would not, but now, at this distance, I regretted it. I did.

Yes, it was nice that after the service, my father had extended his hand to my mother-in-law and said, "So sorry for your loss." But I wasn't surprised at her snub, her turning away from my parents. After all, hadn't they insulted her all those years ago? Hadn't they hurt us all? Were we supposed to forget, to forgive? But that led me to my other regret, another one I needed to atone for.

I WISH I could travel back in time to my phone conversation with my mother after Geoff died. If only I could have the chance to reconsider my words. After I told her when and where the memorial service would be, she asked me, "Do your father and I have to come?"

I remember my answer. I said, "Yes, of course. Of course, you have to come."

I shouldn't have said that even though that's how I felt. Yes, it's true that she and my father had failed to come to our wedding all those years before in Denver. And yes, it felt imperative to me for them to come to Geoff's funeral, almost like a way for them to make up for their past failure. But it was theirs to discover, not mine to impose.

I should have said, "You'll have to decide."

But I was still too angry to be sensitive to their ages; both were eighty-two. Traveling must have been hard for them. And I was ignorant of the progress of my father's prostate cancer. They were good at keeping me in the dark. Now, knowing that my father would die in little more than a year, I feel ashamed.

And yes, they came. And I saw in person how old they were. It was a comfort to have them sit beside me in the cavernous space of the cathedral, to hold their hands. And after the reception, after the egg salad sandwiches and lemonade in the parish hall, it was a rare treat to be able to ask my father to walk back into the beautiful sanctuary and sit together for a few reflective moments.

Perhaps, it was for the best that they came. But I should not have required it of them, fragile as they were.

And I regret my anger, my selfishness.

And I atone for it here. I am sorry.

t w e n t y - o n e

WHAT ABOUT
CHESTER?

n November of 2011, I've just arrived home from spending
Thanksgiving with Simon and his family in Massachusetts. I
phone David from the Downeaster train station. He sounds
awful. I'm worried enough about him that I decide I'll swing by
his apartment before I go home. But it's late; it's getting dark.

I park my Prius in one of the visitor spaces behind David's
apartment building; he likes the downtown Portland vibe
around the city's art museum. A local college student lets me in
the security doors, and I endure the old, creaky elevator. Once
I'm on the fifth floor, I hurry down the hall.

The door to apartment number 511 is unlocked. I call out,
"David, I'm here."

I immediately kneel on the Berber carpeting of the small
living room. Chester, David's cat, runs towards me and accepts
pats on his large yellow head. He purrs loudly, even reaches up
to approximate a kiss near my nose. I scan the apartment's living room and kitchen; dirty cups and glasses clutter every
counter and table. I call out again, "David, I brought you coffee
and banana bread from Starbucks." I set my decaf latte on the
dinette table, throw my parka on the loveseat and fill the sink
with suds and dishes.

"I'm in the bedroom." David's voice sounds weak.

The blinds are drawn, the bedroom, dark. "May I open the shades?" I ask while I move around the room, turning on lights and letting the November gray inside.

While I'm asking, "Have you had anything to eat or drink?" I scoop up a scatter of abandoned T-shirts, boxer shorts, and dirty socks until I have an armful. David's laundry basket in the closet is full so I drop the laundry in the farthest corner from David's bed. Now, at least, a path has been cleared from the bed to the bathroom and from the bedroom to the kitchen.

"How about some orange juice?" I ask. He nods. As fast as a flash, I hand him a juice glass.

I sit down in his desk chair, swivel, and roll close to his bedside. I ask, "How are you? Really?" I study his face. He looks pale. When he strains to sit up, I hear his labored breathing. I've never seen him like this. Chester bounds up on the bed looking for attention, but when David stretches out a hand to stroke the cat's pale yellow fur, his fingers fall short.

"Gotta go to the bathroom," David says. He sits up and staggers across the room. He is so thin that his jeans are half-falling off his hips. "Could you feed Chester?" he asks, not bothering to close the bathroom door. I speed through washing the dishes, filling the dish drainer. I glance down. Chester's food dish, the black and white one, is empty. I fill it with dry food. And give him fresh water.

"You better throw out the old canned food," David calls from the bathroom so I toss it and open a fresh can of Salmon Special Treat while Chester brushes up against my ankles encouraging me to hurry up.

David barely makes it back to his bed. He just falls across it and lies there. He looks more than his seventy-one years. "You're weak." I say to him. "You're sick." I know he hates hospitals and doctors. I think about what he suffered as a young boy. I wait for what seems like a long time.

When David says, "I need to go to the emergency room," I'm more than relieved. "You can drive me," he says. Then he waves a hand at me. "Just give me a little time."

"Okay," I say. I think, *David is a grown man. It's his call. I'm not his girlfriend anymore, just his friend. But I am his friend.* After I witness several of his feeble attempts to walk and several failures, I begin to worry. I wonder, *How will I be able to get him to my car?* The fifth floor hallway is growing longer, the elevator slower, and the security doors heavier. And then I think, *What about the outdoor stairs, the snowy steps down to the parking lot?*

"I don't think I can get you to my car," I say. "I really don't think we should try it."

He nods. He agrees. So I call 911, stay on the line as instructed, provide the correct address including the apartment number. I do my best to describe David's condition—short of breath, slurred speech, weak. *Frail,* I think for the first time. I can hardly believe it. I say it out loud, "He seems frail."

I explain to the person on the other end of the line that David was at the ER on Friday, yes, the Friday after Thanksgiving, and yes, he was sent home. He was told he most likely had bronchitis. But this, this is not bronchitis.

"Yes," I say to the 911 lady, "the front door is unlocked. Yes," I say, "I will put the cat in a closet."

I surprise Chester, pick him up with authority and drop him gently into the crowded walk-in closet. Through the door, I say, "Sorry, Chester."

Lying back on his bed, David looks around his bedroom and says to his bookcases full of loved books and his walls covered with treasured art, "I wonder if I'll ever see you again." I hear him. *What if he's right? What if he senses something?*

I hear sirens; then, I see lights flashing in circles against the storefronts of Congress Street. Four big burly men in bright yellow uniforms arrive; they squeeze through the small entryway, fill the living room and then the bedroom. They are men of action, but they are remarkably polite. They report that the apartment building's elevator is too small for a gurney.

Two of them rush out and quickly return. They produce a bright red metal chair and strap David in, first this way and then that; they tilt the chair back in much the same way that moving men carry boxes of glassware on handcarts. It all happens very fast.

"Here," I say. I pass David his L.L. Bean parka through the tunnel of men. It's cold outside. "Pass me your keys," I say. I'll need them to get into his apartment to take care of Chester.

"Oh, I'll probably be home tomorrow," David says.

I think, *But what if you're not?* All I can bring myself to ask is: "What about Chester?"

DAVID DOESN'T COME home.

t w e n t y - t w o

THE MERRY-GO-
ROUND

When I met my friend, David, in the spring of 2001, he took me to see his art studio. London Stained Glass was at the top of High Street as it rises from the port and intersects with Congress and Free Streets. He worked across from the Portland Museum of Art.

Two walls of windows in David's second floor space offered a clear view of one of Portland's busiest and most iconic corners. Sunlight beamed through the blue, green, and red glass of David's intricate art and splashed color on his walls.

Before I could take more than a step or two inside, David stopped me. He was intent upon showing me a framed calligraphy on the left just inside the door. I could tell by the hushed tone of his voice that he was sharing something important.

He began to read the lyrics of John Lennon's *Watching the Wheels*. Restraining me by an elbow, he read another stanza. David lowered his voice and began to explain how Lennon's song related to his own life. He described himself as a man who had jumped off the merry-go-round of a conventional life. He had left D.C. where he had worked for the CIA; he had left New York City where he worked for Citibank. Never a corporate type, he decided to relocate to Portland after a vacation in Maine. By discovering and developing his latent talent, he went on to create a life of independence and personal integrity.

But in spite of his explanation, I sensed some sadness. I thought how hard it must have been for him to have taken a path different from the one his family had expected and how difficult for him to have given up on his own earlier dreams while he had studied at Dartmouth and then at Johns Hopkins. But I was also struck with how fortunate he had been to have built an enthusiastic following for his work and a circle of art-loving friends.

Several years after I met David, he moved across Congress Street to a newly renovated high-ceilinged studio in a building above the State Theatre. As he settled into his fresh new space on the fifth floor, one of the first steps he took was to place the Lennon calligraphy on the left just inside the door, again in a place of honor.

As HE AGED, David became more bald; his mustache and beard turned more gray, but he remained vigorous. His active work of building stained glass pieces ended, but he collected antique bottles and inkwells and made art with them. Green poison bottles with their ribbed sides and warnings of "DO NOT DRINK" and cobalt blue inkwells added drama to his work. He continued to attend gallery openings, concerts, and lectures, and to host Friday Art Walks in his studio. Several times a year, he took the train to New York City to visit art museums and galleries and to attend flamenco concerts.

The desk in his studio was surrounded by posters of the big city. In his bookcases, he arranged photographs of his Jewish grandparents from Poland beside art books; his favorites were German Expressionism and Rockwell Kent. On the high walls of his studio, he displayed his art museum-style—students' efforts side by side with the work of professional artists. I believe it expressed his philosophy that art enhances the lives of everyone.

When David gave up his art studio and moved down Congress Street into a small apartment, he hung the calligraphy of lyrics in his entryway. His favorite stained glass pieces from over the years glittered high in the windows. But the loveliest sight was to the west above the rooftops of nearby brownstones; on clear days, he could see Mt. Washington.

David's new apartment suited him although he was the oldest resident in a converted college dormitory. He walked up and down the brick and cobblestone streets of Portland greeting artists in their galleries, meeting acquaintances for coffee, and striking up conversations with strangers.

In the last week of his life when David was in the cardiac ICU at Maine Medical Center, I had to accept the reality that he would not be returning home. On a visit to feed his cat, Chester, I took down the calligraphy from his front hallway and gave it to our Unitarian minister along with a beautiful example of David's stained glass. She and David had held lively discussions about how he might become a Unitarian without betraying his Jewish roots. She understood his struggles with his conscience.

When David died, I was struck with how in the end, death is a release from the merry-go-round of life. And so, I thought, *David has jumped off the merry-go-round. Again.*

e p i l o g u e

ON THE OTHER
SIDE

On a Saturday morning in late June in 2014, twenty years after "the lightning accident," I drive out Shore Road to Jordan's Farm in Cape Elizabeth. The strawberry crop is in! I choose a quart and set them carefully in my back seat. I am dreaming of strawberry shortcake as I retrace my route and head for The Buttered Biscuit, a bakery with handy take-out food.

I live in the Willard Beach neighborhood of South Portland, Maine, and I am a regular customer at a triumvirate of three wonderful bakeries—Scratch, The Cookie Jar, and The Buttered Biscuit. At Scratch, where I buy lattes and giant cinnamon rolls, the young staff know me by name; éclairs are my favorite guilty pleasures at The Cookie Jar, and The Buttered Biscuit keeps me in homemade chicken pot pies, also milk between trips to the grocery store.

I park my Prius on a side street and run between oversized raindrops into The Buttered Biscuit. My official errand is to pick up a half-dozen plain biscuits and a pressurized can of whipped cream, but I'm easily distracted. I wander around and study all the possibilities. The salmon teriyaki steaks and string beans with garlic look delicious. And they're healthy. Maybe that's what I should get for dinner.

When I turn around, I'm surprised by the dark sky outside the giant plate glass windows. That's when I notice the heavy rain noisily splashing on the sidewalk outside the bakery's screen door; rain and fog now obscure the neighborhood houses. But it is the thunder that gets my attention.

Ever since Geoff was killed by lightning, and Teddy was badly injured, certain noises—ambulance sirens and thunder, and certain sights—dark skies, torrential rain, and lightning, trigger irrational fear in me. I just want to flee.

While I stare out the windows of the bakery, the lights flicker out and then back on. The owner of the bakery emerges from the kitchen wearing a white apron over his well-fed abdomen; he solemnly closes the front door. A mother who has been shopping with her young son for a treat, a cookie or a brownie, appraises me. And I examine her and the owner just in case we four may be facing an emergency together. The circumstances remind me of being on a plane during a stretch of sustained turbulence when one begins making eye contact and conversation with the passengers across the aisle who may be helpful just in case.

I set my purchases-to-be, a cellophane bag of biscuits and a can of whipped cream, aside. I have lost my appetite for dinner. Maybe later. The owner, a pleasant-faced man with dark wavy hair, remains in the front part of the bakery as though to give us, his customers, courage. As we three adults make comments about the storm, we choose our words carefully so that we will not alarm the little boy, and we speak in tones that are as ordinary as we can make them. But as we watch, the lights in the bakery blink off and then on, then off again with a new kind of finality. And while the rain falls in great sheets from the cruel, dark sky, the thunder seems louder and closer, as though giant footfalls are closing in on the modest shop.

Then it begins, the lightning. Flashes we can see through

the windows. Flashes that are unpredictable and suggest chaos. Flashes that also seem more numerous and spectacular. I have been in the shop now for what feels like a long time, and I have a strong impulse to hurry home. "I might as well go," I say to the bakery owner and the mother and child.

I will get sopping wet, but I will run, and once I am in my car, I will be safe. And then, I will drive home. Home sounds so attractive. I pull up the hood of my windbreaker, not rainproof.

"No," the owner says with a tone more serious than I expect. "Not now," he says with authority *and* kindness. "*Now* is not a good time." And a series of claps of thunder confirm his wisdom. The lightning crackles around the little hillside the bakery sits on.

"Well," I say and then exhale a "Whew." I am glad to remain inside the darkened shop with the owner, who seems to have assumed the role of protector. I suppose that responsibility comes along with the feeding of his neighbors.

The rest of the story is just as you would expect. The thunder and lightning travel on up the hill toward Meeting House Church and its cemetery. The worst of the storm moves away. I make one more premature feint to leave the shop. "I should go," I say with a hint of a question mixed in with my statement.

The owner asks, "Why not wait till the rain lets up?" A sensible question. And about then, the lights come back on. Life in the bakery returns to normal. I choose a salmon steak and green beans for my dinner. The cash register clicks into action adding up my dinner and fixings for strawberry shortcake. I am surprised to realize how hungry I am.

The owner opens the front door, and I say, "Thank you." And I shake his hand. My "thank you" is for the good food and for his interventions on behalf of my safety. And for his kindness. I include a great deal in my simple words, "Thank you."

Outdoors, the rain has stopped and the sky is light gray. As I drive down Cottage Road and make the left turn onto Pillsbury Street, a rainbow appears. I swear it does. And as I enter Willard Square, an oddly shaped intersection left over from the days of trolleys, and turn left toward home, my car and I drive through the arc of the rainbow. I swear we do. I pass through the rainbow until I am on the other side.

I think, *I am on the other side. I really am.*

Readers have asked me about how my sons, especially my younger son, fared after the lightning accident. I can assure them that both of my sons continued with their educations, found meaningful professions, and are happily married with children.

My younger son, the one who was badly hurt, recovered over time. Eventually, he was able to resume undergraduate school; he graduated five years after the accident in 1999. The same year, he ran in the Marine Corps Marathon in Washington D.C. He married the pretty nurse I mention in *The Red Ribbon* and immediately went on to graduate school at Quinnipiac University in Connecticut. For many years, he worked as a physician's assistant at Hartford Children's Hospital in its emergency room. Recently, he moved to a small private practice near his home in southern Connecticut.

My older son is a psychiatric nurse practitioner who works in a clinic setting in Massachusetts. He and his wife just celebrated a milestone wedding anniversary. Both of my sons and their families enjoy outdoor activities especially skiing, biking, and hiking. I am fortunate that we all live in New England and are able to share vacations and holidays.

ACKNOWLEDGMENTS

First, I wish to acknowledge the debt that I owe to my parents who both loved books; my mother's preference was English Literature and my father, history and biography. They raised a daughter who enjoys and values a well-written book.

I began writing memoir at the University of Southern Maine in 2000; I wish to thank my professor, Dianne Benedict, for her encouragement. Later, I joined the Osher Lifelong Learning Institute (OLLI) at USM. I took intermediate and advanced memoir writing classes with Ruth Story and participated in her memoir writing workshop. I also pursued fiction writing classes with Tim Baehr and joined Denney Morton's fiction writing workshop. Tim copy-edited *The Red Ribbon*, and Denney was one of my most valued readers.

I am indebted to Ruth Story; she began as my teacher, then became my mentor, and finally, my friend. From Ruth, I learned Anne Lamott's *Bird by Bird* method of constructing a longer work. Ruth was the one who suggested that I create a book from my shorter memoir pieces. She edited *The Red Ribbon*.

For many years, my "writing buddy," Joan Kotz, has been available to read my work whether a rough draft or a piece in need of polishing. I wish to express my gratitude. I am fortunate to have such a good friend.

I have benefitted from being a member of the Portland area OLLI, now a community of over 2200 students and teachers fifty years of age or older. Within OLLI, a group of committed writers flourishes. I value my fellow writers; they have provided thoughtful feedback and ideas. In particular, I wish to thank Barbara Kautz, Jane Ann McNeish, and Anne and George Ball for being early readers of my manuscript. Thank you to three

OLLI poets, Judith Manion, Janet Stebbins, and Muriel Allen, who read my poetry and prose. And thanks to Paul Kiley, another OLLI teacher whose feedback was helpful. And thank you to Christine Linnehan, my therapist, for her support and for providing a professional's perspective.

I have also been lucky to be a member of the MWPA, the Maine Writers and Publishers Alliance. Two of their harvest workshops in Kennebunkport were especially helpful; I am thankful for the guidance of Monica Wood and Meredith Hall. The 2016 Stonecoast Summer Conference was another super experience; my thanks to Elizabeth Peavcy. And I appreciate the time the director of MPWA, Joshua Bodwell, spent with me discussing publishing options including She Writes Press. And thank you to the publisher of She Writes Press, Brooke Warner, and my editorial manager, Samantha Strom; I knew I was in good hands from the beginning. And special thanks to my talented and supportive publicist, Caitlin Hamilton Summie. I have been fortunate.

Books that have formed the bedrock of my education about grief are Judith Viorst's *Necessary Losses,* C. S. Lewis' *A Grief Observed,* and Joan Dideon's *The Year of Magical Thinking.*

Thank you to all my fellow writers, friends, and family who I have not mentioned individually; each of you contributed to my completed manuscript. And finally thank you to my wonderful sons who traveled their own path of grief and still have had love left over to support me.

Thank you.

NANCY FREUND BILLS, a native of Montana, has lived almost all her adult life in northern New England. She is currently on the faculty of the Osher Lifelong Learning Institute at the University of Southern Maine, OLLI/USM, where she facilitates the fiction writing workshop. She is a retired clinical social worker; during her twenty year long career, she served both as a psychiatric social worker at Concord Regional Hospital in New Hampshire and at Maine Medical Center in Portland, Maine, and as a psychotherapist at Green House Group, a group private practice in Manchester, New Hampshire.

Out of six thousand entries, Chapter 19, "The Myth," received first place in the memoir/personal essay category of the 83rd Annual *Writer's Digest* Writing Competition. Out of one thousand entries, Chapter 14, "Triage and Cows," made the Top 25 list in *Glimmer Train's* Very Short Fiction competition in July/August 2016. Bills' memoir, fiction and poetry have been published in *Reflections, the Maine Review, the LLI Review, the Goose River Anthology,* and in the *83rd Annual Writer's Digest Writing Competition Collection.*

Bills received an MS in twentieth century literature and art from the University of Rochester and an MSW in clinical social work from the University of Connecticut. She and her two Maine Coon cats live on the southern coast of Maine. This is her first full-length memoir.

SELECTED TITLES FROM SHE WRITES PRESS

She Writes Press is an independent publishing company
founded to serve women writers everywhere.
Visit us at www.shewritespress.com.

Naked Mountain: A Memoir by Marcia Mabee. $16.95,
978-1-63152-097-6. A compelling memoir of one woman's journey
of natural world discovery, tragedy, and the enduring bonds of
marriage, set against the backdrop of a stunning mountaintop in
rural Virginia.

Rethinking Possible: A Memoir of Resilience by Rebecca Faye Smith
Galli. $16.95, 978-1-63152-220-8. After her brother's devastatingly
young death tears her world apart, Becky Galli embarks upon a quest
to recreate the sense of family she's lost—and learns about healing
and the transformational power of love over loss along the way.

Green Nails and Other Acts of Rebellion: Life After Loss by Elaine
Soloway. $16.95, 978-1-63152-919-1. An honest, often humorous
account of the joys and pains of caregiving for a loved one with a
debilitating illness.

Painting Life: My Creative Journey Through Trauma by Carol K.
Walsh. $16.95, 978-1-63152-099-0. Carol Walsh was a
psychotherapist working with traumatized clients when she
encountered her own traumatic experience; this is the story of how
she used creativity and artistic expression to heal, recreate her life,
and ultimately thrive.

All Set for Black, Thanks: A New Look at Mourning by Miriam
Weinstein. $16.95, 978-1-63152-109-6. A wry, irreverent take on
how we mourn, how we remember, and how we keep our dead with
us even as we (sort of) let them go.

Four Funerals and a Wedding: Resilience in a Time of Grief by Jill
Smolowe. $16.95, 978-1-938314-72-8. When journalist Jill Smolowe
lost four family members in less than two years, she turned to
modern bereavement research for answers—and made some
surprising discoveries.